WOMAN'S HOUR

WOMAN'S HOUR

Words from wise, witty
and wonderful women

Foreword by Jenni Murray

1 3 5 7 9 10 8 6 4 2

BBC Books, an imprint of Ebury Publishing
20 Vauxhall Bridge Road,
London SW1V 2SA

BBC Books is part of the Penguin Random House group
of companies whose addresses can be found at
global.penguinrandomhouse.com

Penguin
Random House
UK

Copyright © Woodlands Books 2017

First published by BBC Books in 2017

www.penguin.co.uk

ISBN 9781785942426

Printed and bound in Great Britain by Clays Ltd, St Ives PLC

Penguin Random House is committed to a sustainable future
for our business, our readers and our planet. This book is
made from Forest Stewardship Council® certified paper.

MIX
Paper from
responsible sources
FSC® C018179

CONTENTS

FOREWORD BY JENNI MURRAY

It's been such a pleasure for me to read through these wonderfully wise and witty words and remember all the extraordinary women I've been privileged to encounter in the past thirty years. Yes, it has been that long. My younger son, who is about to turn thirty, doesn't remember me being anything but Mum, the *Woman's Hour* presenter!

Of course the programme is much older. We celebrated her seventieth birthday in October last year. I was born in 1950, four years after the first edition, and became a listener at my mother's breast. Feeding schedules in those days were strictly four-hourly and 2 o'clock in the afternoon – the time of transmission until 1993 when we moved to the morning – was perfect for the mother who'd had her lunch, put up her feet and put her baby to her breast.

I must have heard so many of the women in this book because I was a fan of the programme long before I joined. I remember hearing Enid Blyton talking about being forced to play the piano as a child when all she wanted to do was write. I was so impressed by her, and George in *The Famous Five* is still one of my favourite characters.

I doubt I heard Nancy Astor saying her husband's wealth was one of the reasons she married him. I would have loved to have interviewed her, she had such a sense of humour, but that interview took place in 1956 when I was only six and hadn't yet cottoned on to the significance of the first woman to take her seat in the British Parliament.

The subject matter included in this volume is as wide-ranging as the women and their interests. Whether it's politics or knitting, breast cancer or baking a beautiful cake, these are experiences we all share. We all grew up as little girls, we all worried about family and children – whether we were able to have them or not – we all experience love and relationships and grapple with health and lifestyle issues and I doubt there's a woman in the world who hasn't agonised over her body image. It's always surprised me that even the most beautiful never see in the mirror what we see on the screen. Jane Fonda, when she was encouraging us all to 'feel the burn' with her fitness videos, explained on *Woman's Hour* that her father, Henry, had always made her feel she was fat.

Some of the women in this book sat across from me in the studio or I met them in their own homes and I will never forget them and what they had to say. Benazir Bhutto had suffered the execution of her father, exile in England and was planning her return to Pakistan to begin her career in politics. We sat in her aunt's flat in London as she explained that she had trusted her mother to choose a husband for her. A young, unmarried woman wouldn't stand a chance in public life in Pakistan. She was the first woman to lead a Muslim-majority nation and was Prime Minister twice. Her assassination in 2007 touched me deeply.

I met Carly Simon in her house in Boston as part of a special programme about the city. She refused to tell me which of her lovers she'd described as 'so vain' but talked about her treatment for breast cancer with a sense of humour I've found to be quite common among women who've had to deal with the disease – 'I think having two breasts was overrated anyway,' she said.

Among the most memorable conversations about children and grandchildren were with Hillary Clinton, who admitted finding it hard to muddle through her career as a new mum with a new baby, and Doris Lessing who had left two of her children behind when she escaped her marriage in Africa and raised her remaining son alone in London. It was more difficult, she thought, to bring up a boy without a father than it would have been to raise a daughter.

Then there was Shirley Williams, one of my favourite interviewees of all time, on her grandsons with whom she tried to spend as much time as possible, but 'they too have had to adapt to the idea of not only young women working, but much older women working until they drop'.

My absolute favourite comment though came from Oprah Winfrey on her difficulties with yo-yo dieting. 'What kind of life is it without a French fry ever?' Definitely a woman after my own heart.

If you're a mother, daughter, grandmother, sister, aunt, wife, partner, friend, young or old there'll be something in this book to delight you. Enjoy!

Jenni Murray
February 2017

GROWING UP

As Julie Andrews famously sang, 'Let's start at the beginning, a very good place to start.'

The diversity of the eminent guests on Woman's Hour *is never more evident than in their varied backgrounds and upbringings and it's those very beginnings that shaped them into the wise and wonderful women they are today.*

'I've been in show business for an awful long time. As I say, I was a child sort of prodigy or whatever you care to call it. I think that touring a lot, as I did when I was young, gave me a great deal of discipline.'

**Actress and *Sound of Music* star
Julie Andrews, 1974**

'I had a blissful childhood, because I loved Pembrokeshire, and my brother and I more or less ran wild, over the cliffs and studying the birds and scrambling. We would take off from morning and just appear after dark.

'The War was on and we were being shunted from one school to another and I managed to escape school for whole summers on end. My father [was] involved with a boys' school, so I went to a boys' school at one stage, which was quite fun. I was a sort of pet, a sort of mascot.'

Mary Quant recalling her Welsh childhood in 1971

'I was very earnest when I was fourteen. I thought I was the only one who really understood the ills of the world. I was the only one really feeling it.'

Harry Potter **author JK Rowling, 2000**

Author Enid Blyton had been a cornerstone of children's literature since the 1930s but in 1963 she told Woman's Hour *her family had other plans for her talents.*

'My father always wanted me to be a musician. Music is in my family. I had a very clever aunt who used to give concerts and things like that, and my father rather visualised that I would do the same. Therefore at six years old, I had to begin to learn to play the piano and all through my childhood, there was practice, practice, practice 'til I was in my teens, when I was doing four hours a day.

'Now, if you have to work at something that you have really no desire to achieve anything great in, it becomes a terrible bore. And all the time I still wanted to write.'

Children's author Enid Blyton, 1963

'I was in the theatre from the time I was five until I was twelve, and at twelve I was over five feet tall and it was difficult getting jobs acting as a child. The films had a great problem, their photography was so bad.

'They really needed the youngest kind of faces. Once we used a baby and we saw it on the screen and had to send back to the orphanage where the little one came from and say, "Please send us a young-looking baby!" So I was twelve when I went into films, and played heroines from the time I was twelve until I was seventeen, and then an old hag of eighteen goes into character work and she plays mothers. And by the time I was thirty, I was finished with my film career and back in the theatre.'

Hollywood legend Lillian Gish, 1957

———◆———

'My grandmother had a piano that somehow got to our house, but to start with it was a little toy piano that I had when I was very tiny, about three, and my mother realised I could pick tunes out. I guess if someone is gifted musically, it should really show. She said I used to sing myself to sleep when I was young.'

Annie Lennox

'Nowadays people do not have unwanted children, at least not very many people have them. The children they have they really want and they really love, and it's a totally different affair from when I was a child. I lived in a poor neighbourhood and there were many families with twelve and fourteen children they couldn't feed. These children were not exactly loved, wanted little creatures. They were not wanted, and everybody treated children, especially boys, but even girls, as bad. Children were bad by nature. It was just nature. You had to beat it out of them, and most families did. The fact that my family didn't made them really an anomaly in our neighbourhood.'

American author Marilyn French, 2006

———◆◦◆———

'I thought when I was little that honey came from bees. I picked one up and I got stung on my tongue. I must have been quite small. But I remember picking it up and it stung my tongue. It was awful and I screamed and screamed.'

***The Great British Bake Off* star
Mary Berry, 2016**

'At the age of six, I was in bed with the measles. I've never really lived down the disgrace of it, but I cut up a bedspread to try and make myself a dress in a completely new shape. It was a bit of a disaster. I used the nail scissors.'

Mary Quant gives an insight into the early years of a fashion design icon

'The newspaper in our town was done by whites, and my grandmother said "for whites and about whites". And any time they mentioned anybody black, it was something terrible about the person. You know, that person has stolen something, or robbed or raped or killed, or something terrible. And we had a normal town with very little violence and the people worked hard, black people worked hard, white people worked hard. But the white newspaper did not report that.

'But once a month, there would be a women's page in the white newspaper, and my grandmother would ask one of the maids who passed by her store, she'd say, "Sister Hudson, will you bring me the page this time?" and the maid would get the page and bring it back. My grandmother and I would pore over it.

'We had two paraffin lamps and I would sit there with her and we would take every recipe out of the page and then my grandmother would fold it up, give it to the maid, the maid would take it back to her work, press it, iron it, and put it back in the newspaper, and the white woman for whom she worked wouldn't even know the page had been gone.'

Author Maya Angelou

Singer Helen Shapiro shot to fame in 1961 at the age of fourteen, with the huge hits 'Walkin' Back to Happiness' and 'Don't Treat Me Like a Child'. Twelve years later she told Woman's Hour *how childhood stardom affected her.*

'My friends always treated me exactly the same as ever and my school friends too. Teachers changed a little towards me and started picking on me a little bit but I suppose they did this to keep my feet on the ground. In the end, we got on OK. Private life, all my friends at that time were starting to go from the youth club up to the West End to all the clubs and this I missed. But it didn't bother me too much because I was starting to travel and this was an ambition of mine and to me, it made up for everything, I was seeing the world.'

Helen Shapiro, 1973

'I wish I had been a teenager. But when I was that age the concept didn't exist, or if it did it didn't come my way. So I never wore my hair in a pony-tail, or danced to rock n' roll until I was ready to drop, or wore drainpipe trousers (not then, anyway), or shrieked when I saw pictures of film stars or wore bright pink luminous socks. I dare say I was well enough off without the shrieking and the socks, but the rest I regret.'

Author Iris Murdoch, 1957

'When Jim [Threapleton] and I got married, in his speech that he made, my dad said, "If any of you know Kate, you'll know that she goes at things" and he was talking about when my mum gave birth to me and I shot out like, "Yes, I've arrived, I'm here." And I don't know, I think I've just always been a very strong-headed, determined person and also I spend my whole life thinking we've got one life, what is there really to lose?'

Actress Kate Winslet, 2000

'Have a try and also be kind to yourself. I look back at the very angst-ridden girl I was at sixteen, and I just wish I could have given myself a break. It's such a tough time. I think "be who you are" is really the best advice for a teenager. Be who you are. There's so much pressure on you from everyone to be something else. You need to find out who you are, and then as Dolly Parton famously said, "Do it on purpose."'

JK Rowling

———◆◆◆———

'I was always tall – I was this tall when I was eleven – so I was never physically bullied but I went to a girls' school and girls aren't always nice to each other. But I was such a loser as a kid that I had people taking me under their wing. I got the opposite of bullying because I looked so hopeless. I was always getting into trouble because I was late and I was just a basket case. What I elicited was not bullying but pity!'

**Actress Sigourney Weaver, 2016,
who stands at almost 6ft**

In 1975, after a decade of modelling, Twiggy was asked what she had been like ten years earlier, when she was still known as Lesley Hornby.

'Just an ordinary girl from Neasden. I was at school. I left school in the middle of the term to try the modelling thing. It could've all fallen through in a month but I was lucky, it didn't.

'My headmistress wasn't very pleased actually. Obviously I had to have my dad's permission to leave and he was great because he said, "It may be a mistake, it may be a flash in the pan but if I stop you, you'll probably end up hating me for the rest of your life because you'd always wonder what would've happened."'

Twiggy, 1975

'I was brought up on this farm with the women at one end and the men at the other rubbishing each other. Men have to rubbish women if they're stuck in a farming district, they have to rubbish them to somebody, and women have to say men are terrible, and so this is what I was used to as a girl. You see, feminism didn't start till the Sixties.'

Author Doris Lessing, 2008

———•••———

'When I was brought up there wasn't much sense of difference between the brothers and the sisters and therefore I never felt that as a woman I had to prove myself.'

Benazir Bhutto, Prime Minister of Pakistan, 1989

Drew Barrymore became a household name at the age of seven, when she starred in ET. *Her teenage years were marred with drug and alcohol abuse and at fourteen she wrote her memoir,* Little Girl Lost, *which she followed in 2015 with a book of autobiographical essays,* Wildflower. *She appeared on* Woman's Hour *in 2007.*

'I think it was just like every young person has to figure out who they are, find out what they want to be, what they don't want to be. What they want to do, what they don't want to do. I was a bit younger because I had to grow up so fast because of my job and it was obviously more public than some people have experienced it. But it's just the same feeling. And it's the same experience, and it's the same emotion that everybody goes through which is growing pains and falling on your face and picking yourself back up again. I think every human being on the planet has experienced that. So I'm certainly no different. What a wonderful adventure, nonetheless, for me. And it's something I'm very proud of and I wouldn't be who I am today without it.'

Drew Barrymore

'I would have loved to have been a modern expression ballerina. That was really my sort of passion – dance. And regrettably, my father kept on telling me that I had a brain and that I had to use it. I tried to persuade him it was a very small brain, but he wasn't convinced.'

Baroness Scotland, the first black woman to be appointed as a QC. She received a peerage in 1997 and later served as a minister in Tony Blair's cabinet

'I was born during the War, and my mother sewed. She made our clothes. And we used to go walking round the reservoir to a lady who lived in a remote cottage, to get coats made. And we used to have a Christmas pantomime at the church, and my mother was always making clothes for that. So there was a sewing machine in our little cottage, which converted into a table if you wanted. And I was sewing dolls clothes as a child, making models. Always sewing. Learned to knit. So then I made my clothes as a teenager. As a young person, I spent my money on shoes and made all my clothes.'

Dame Vivienne Westwood on learning to sew, 2014

'At fourteen I left school to stay at home and help Mum but I soon tired of having nothing much to do, so I decided to go into business on my own. I bought an outfit for leather-making and did a roaring trade with my family and friends with bags, purses and wallets. But when they were satisfied, there were no more customers so I decided to look for a job dressmaking.'

Dame Vera Lynn, 1950

Travel writer Freya Stark had an unconventional upbringing, exploring new territories with her adventurous parents.

'One just looked at a map of Europe and had no passports to think about and no currency questions and went wherever one liked … We were carried across the Dolomites, my sister and I, when I was about two and a half, by the guides, so that we began very early. I think travel was taken in one's stride rather in those days.'

Freya Stark, 1965

'When I was in the third form I came thirty-first in maths out of a class of thirty-two. In the fourth form I came tenth out of the same class, because I'd persuaded a girl on the next desk to do my homework. I didn't like her. I never gave her anything in return. I don't even remember her name. But she was my rung up the ladder that would take me to the swankiest class in the fifth form. So I telephoned her ever night and picked her brains with a hatchet.'

Journalist Jean Rook muses on her fierce ambition in 1965

In 1976, the then leader of the Conservative Party, Margaret Thatcher, told Woman's Hour *about growing up in Grantham, a small town in Lincolnshire, and living above her father's grocery store.*

'I think the main difference between then and now is that in those days, of course, there was no television, although we had a radio when I was about ten. I can remember the day when it arrived. And so you had to make a lot of your own amusement.

'Also in my life we used to do a lot of talking and discussing. Inevitably, being part of a shop, we knew a lot of people. They came in, we chatted. Because we lived over the shop people would often call. In a church background, we attended lots of church meetings. So I was brought up with a background of discussion.'

Margaret Thatcher, 1976

'I always enjoyed talking to strangers. When I was eighteen months old my mother used to be deeply embarrassed by the fact that I used to wink at strangers from the pram.'

TV presenter Esther Rantzen, 1978

FAMILY TIES

From grandparents and parents to children and grandchildren, the family plays a huge part in the lives of women. Over the years the subject has thrown up some fascinating stories and amazing insights into the very different backgrounds of the show's guests.

'The family is the building brick of the community and its strength, and every child is entitled to a good family life.'

Margaret Thatcher, 1993

———◆·◆·◆———

'Quite honestly, my horses meant more to me than close family members.'

**Jenny Pitman, the first female trainer
to win the Grand National**

'My mother was an incredible woman but she wasn't a stage mum at all. She worked very hard to give me money to go to school and without her belief, it's possible I might not have pursued this, but she always had the belief that I would do something unusual and she thought that this [acting] was the area for me. I guess she was right.'

Actress Bette Davis, 1979

———◆◆◆———

'I was my father's daughter. I followed in his footsteps, listened to his songs and everything he had to say. There were careers to me would have been obscene.

'I was made in 1926 when I saw the suffering imposed on people who had been my chums at school, my friends. We didn't suffer, in a sense of hunger, having to take a bowl to a soup kitchen, but I was so infuriated. What was done to the miners in 1926 shaped the whole of my future life.'

Labour politician Jennie Lee, speaking in 1980 about her father, former miner James Lee

'I think I should say that in the last number of years, my parents are both 93 years old, I have a granddaughter who's three, my son's 36 and his wife is in the picture as well, and I have spent time with them. My son got chipped out of a lot of my time when he was little, and I want to spend family time while there's still a chance. So I've done a lot of that and it tends to get looked over because I am seen as a protest person.'

US singer and activist Joan Baez

Margaret Atwood grew up in Canada and spent much of her time in the wilderness with her mother and father, a forest entomologist. When she spoke to Woman's Hour *in 1987, her mother was in her late seventies and admirably active, skiing and skating every day.*

'Not only does [my mother] ice-skate but she does ice-skate dancing, and was therefore very interested in Torvill and Dean. That's her field ... She never very much liked being indoors and sweeping the floor and doing things like that. She would much rather be outside, which was probably why it was a successful marriage because she really quite liked being up in the wilderness, although it might be other people's vision of hell to be in the woods surrounded by bears and mosquitoes with two small children under the age of three. But she quite took to it.'

Margaret Atwood

'One of the main things my mother did as a mother ... she was not great at hardcore mothering, but she was great at giving us books to read. We were bookworms. We loved children's books.'

Director Nora Ephron, the daughter of screenwriters Henry and Phoebe Ephron, on the upbringing that led her and her three sisters Delia, Amy and Haillie into writing careers

———◆◆◆———

'My great grandmother ended up in the workhouse because her eighth child was illegitimate. She ended up losing her children, and her family, because of that. Now people are choosing to have the sexual life they want on their terms, the children they want on their terms and that's where we are now. But we are still trying to please and be pleasing to people. There's something about us, as females, that we have to be accepted, and I think a lot of it is accepted with our own sex. It's our journey and our choice that we have to work on, not the opposition.'

Actress Felicity Kendal, 2016

'I wasn't mothered well. I know there are lots of people who weren't mothered well and that makes them have the desire to do it, but I never felt I could make up for not being mothered. I always felt that I don't know how to do that.'

**Chat show host and actress
Oprah Winfrey, 1999**

-·-·◆·-·-

'We were eleven in our family, and my father was a symbol of authority, both because of his role in the family as a father, and the fact that he was our school principal. We never, for instance, had the warm, affectionate relationship other children I observed in later life had with their parents. When my father walked into the room where we were, we stood up until he left the room. We never sat on his lap, we never played with him, we never really enjoyed the warmth of a family relationship.'

Winnie Mandela, former wife of South African activist Nelson Mandela, speaking in 1986

Benazir Bhutto's father Zulfikar was Prime Minister of Pakistan for two years before being deposed and later hanged in a military coup in 1973.

'My father never ever said to me, "I am ambitious for you". In fact, he wanted each of us to do whatever we wanted in our lives, as long as it was something worthwhile. What motivates me now is certainly I am inspired by him and what he wanted to do for Pakistan. And not just what he wanted me to do, but what he wanted every young Pakistani to come forward and do for their country.'

Benazir Bhutto, 1988

'My mum has been the sort of mother that I needed and I hope I do the same for my kids. We have lots of communication, we have lots of fun, we spend lots of time together – probably a slightly sickening amount – but I also like the fact that we have quite a clear dynamic in that my mum never wanted to be my best buddy. She wanted to be my mum.'

Sophie Ellis-Bextor, 2016, on mum Janet Ellis

'[My grandfather] came as a spoilt and elegant and probably arrogant member of the upper classes in Russia and finished up as a taxi driver not too many years later. And certainly my family struggled economically at the beginning of my life. They had to make do and survive. Many immigrants come out of poverty and that's the reason that they are leaving their country and they work and they do well and they achieve. In my family's case, it rather went the other way!'

**Dame Helen Mirren speaking in 2007
on her upper-class Russian grandfather,
who emigrated to Britain under Stalin's rule**

———◆———

'I'm a grandmother, I'm an extremely busy grandmother, and so my grandchildren, whom I adore, don't expect to see me every day. They're pleased when they do, but they too have had to adapt to the idea of not only young women working, but much older women working until they drop.'

Baroness Shirley Williams, 2004

'After twenty-two years of studying, I couldn't pay for
my lessons because they were too expensive, so I had to
get a job in a bar, and that's when I changed my name to
Nina Simone. My mother and father would have hated me
if they thought that I was playing in a bar and they would
have killed me, so I just had to change my name so they
wouldn't know ... [when they found out] They didn't like
it at all. They still do not like me playing in nightclubs and
bars. They only like me giving concerts.'

**Preacher's daughter Nina Simone, born
Eunice Kathleen Waymon, on changing her
name to launch a singing career her parents
disapproved of**

------◆◆◆------

*Drew Barrymore had a turbulent relationship with her parents,
John and Jaid, and later said she believed they never wanted
children.*

'It's the way they behaved at times that would lead me
to believe that. But, ultimately, we all have great love
for each other. I think there's a lot of love and respect
there. But some families are more dysfunctional than
others. Ours was quite. And I don't think I've ever found
a completely normal family yet to this day. Family is an
interpretive thing. It's what you make it.'

Drew Barrymore

'It started at the get-go with chocolate advent calendars. I was never allowed a chocolate advent calendar when I was a kid.'

Sophie Ellis-Bextor reveals the difference between Janet Ellis as a mum and as a grandmother

———◆———

At fifteen, Drew Barrymore successfully sued for legal emancipation from her mother, Jaid. The pair were later reconciled.

'Sometimes you have to take a time-out from people in life. I don't think you should beat yourself up too much for that. Sometimes some maturing and watering and nurturing of the garden is sort of important to make it regrow when you've burnt it down, so to speak.

'As I grow and get older, I maintain the relationships of my life, and that includes my mother.'

Drew Barrymore

When author Isabel Allende's son split from the mother of his three children, she set about finding him a wife. In 2008, she told Woman's Hour *about her quest.*

'I saw my son was alone, not dating. Very handsome, by the way, and very charming, and I thought, what a waste. And so I went out to find a bride. Mothers in India do that so I said, "why not". Of course, in California it's very hard to do that.

'I didn't want to place ads in newspapers because I had not as yet asked Nicolas. But I did find a wife and they have been married for eleven very happy years. So, as a matchmaker, I did a good job.

'I needed to test her in a brief time. So I had a trip to the Amazon and decided to take her. I had only seen her once in a restaurant over sushi. And we ended up in the Amazon in a very stressful trip. And she passed all the tests so then I introduced her to my son.'

Isabel Allende

'My mother was very beautiful, very over the top, she ran an excellent business and she was very much the breadwinner. I didn't know until 1969 that you were supposed to take men seriously.'

Journalist and broadcaster Anne Robinson, 2001

'I have had a lot of change in my life and I have had to start from scratch many times in different places in different languages. And I have had to put together a family many times. I know that at this point I have this little tribe in California, and I adore them. And I wish I was like the godfather and I could have a compound with bodyguards so they could never get out. But that's not how it's going to be. Now I have a grandson that is going to college, and my granddaughter will soon be out also. The dynamics change. Everybody moves. And who knows? In ten years I may be all by myself. And I don't want people to take care of me. That is what scares me the most – dependency.'

Isabel Allende

As a teenager Welsh singer Shirley Bassey was discovered singing in a working men's club and asked to audition for a show in London, Memories of Jolson.

'My mother kept pushing me and said, "Go on." She said, "Have a go at it." I didn't like it at first, being away from home for the first time, and being so far away from home alone. I kept writing home to say I didn't like it and she kept writing letters back to say, "Stick it out." Really it was her that kept me going.'

Shirley Bassey, 1957

'When my mother was quite a small girl they moved to Jaipur, which had a great deal of *Purdah* – seclusion of women. Her uncle was the chief minister of the state and he felt that it would be very undignified for a girl of twelve or thirteen to go out with her face exposed: she was supposed to stay at home and be ladylike. Well, my mother had been rather a tomboy because she had two brothers, so this didn't suit her and she became pale and ill-looking. My grandmother found a way out, without telling my grandfather or the rest of my family. That was by dressing my mother as a boy and hiding her pigtail in a turban so that she could go out with the boys and retain her health and complexion.'

Indira Gandhi, 1962

———•◆•———

'I was very fortunate in having the father I had. His father was a jockey and my dad always had ponies for us. He was a farmer and we were by no means a wealthy family – there were seven of us – but my dad always had time for us where the horses were concerned.'

Jenny Pitman, the first woman to train a Grand National winner, speaking in 1981

'My dad was a Communist really but he was very young. He was certainly a leftwing Socialist all of his life. I think he let go of Communism when he realised the kind of abuses that had existed under Bolshevism in Russia. When that penny finally dropped, he was very disappointed as many of those idealistic young Communists had been. But it was a very different world that my dad grew up in, the Western world of the 1920s, it was the rise of Socialism and unionism and it was needed, it was necessary. And certainly Diana Mosley and many others of the British aristocracy were moving quite vehemently towards Fascism.'

Dame Helen Mirren

'[My father] saw me the first time he'd ever been to a theatre in his life. It was when I was playing at Cardiff New Theatre and he came to the opening night and he was so pleased and went home and said, "Missus" – he called my mother "Missus" – "Missus," he said, "I've got a programme of your daughter," and my mother opened the programme and it was the following week's programme.'

Shirley Bassey, 1957

'My mother was very scathing of people that label their children – "the clever one", "the singer", etc. – because that doesn't give you any freedom to be anything else at all. I had that as a watchword with my children and they then constantly surprise me with what they want to do.'

TV presenter Janet Ellis, 2016

MOTHERHOOD AND CHILDREN

Becoming a mother is one of the most momentous changes in any woman's life and not one that everyone chooses. But inevitably parenting and children are recurring themes in the Woman's Hour *studio.*

'I was worried because I had never been a mother before and one night when [Chelsea] was crying, as babies do, I said, "You've never been a baby before and I've never been a mother. We're just going to have to work together and figure this out." But it was the greatest experience of my life and I adored being her mother.'

Former First Lady Hillary Clinton had her only child, Chelsea, in 1980 at the age of 33. In 2003 she spoke to *Woman's Hour* about being a new mother.

Margaret Thatcher was elected as a Conservative MP in 1959 when her twins, Carol and Mark, were six.

'I didn't become a Member of Parliament until after my children had started to go to school because I think that when they're very young they need Mum and Mum certainly needs to be with them. The years nought to five are important years. I hope the children would have missed me and I should certainly have missed them.'

Margaret Thatcher, 1976

'I think the reliance on nature to do the right thing by women is a terribly misguided one. If we relied on nature we'd all be dying in childbirth at 29 and always pregnant. I just don't think nature is to be trusted.'

Julie Burchill, 1999

Chat show host Oprah Winfrey is child-free and in 1999
she explained how she had finally learned that was the right
decision for her

'I was left with my godchild, Katie Rose, for a day. I've
always said parenting, and mothering especially, is the
hardest job in the world. I was left with a four-year-old
for a day. I was so exhausted and stressed out, so grateful
to her mum for coming to get her, that I finally answered
that question, "Should I have had children?"

'I had been questioning that because I thought there might
come a day when I regretted it, and I think every woman
goes through that at some point, and I realised that I made
the right choice for myself. The energy and spirit that it takes
to be a good mother is not something I believe that I have.

'At the end of the day I felt like I had resolved that for
myself because I couldn't do that every day, and do it well.'

Oprah Winfrey

———◆◆◆———

'I watch my daughter Emma, and all the generation now
and parenting has become like a competitive sport. The
self-help industry doesn't function financially unless young
mothers are persuaded that it's difficult to bring up
children and they need help.'

Anne Robinson, 2016

'I take my hat off to women today, some of whom have two or three children, and still manage to stay married and to have very satisfactory and very advanced political careers. But let us not kid ourselves, usually somebody either suffers or is pulled in as a second wife. Let's take Cherie Blair, who I greatly admire. I think nevertheless it's crucial that her mother is a very substantial part of that family. The *babushka* position, if you like, the grandmother, who is indispensable, and I think it would have been very difficult for the Blairs to do all they do – and they do an immense amount – had there not been that extremely committed and obviously very caring lady at the centre of their family.'

Baroness Shirley Williams, 2004

At the end of 2016, TV presenter Janet Ellis and her singer daughter, Sophie Ellis-Bextor appeared on a special show about the mother-daughter relationship. Janet was asked how she felt about being pregnant with Sophie at 23.

Janet: 'I felt enormously clever. I thought "This is so clever of me to have got pregnant, and to be having a baby." I managed to sustain that for quite a long time. Of course the reality was that when she was born I felt as nervous as any new mother.'

Jenni: 'What kind of mother was she, Sophie?'

Sophie: 'Very clever!'

Janet Ellis and Sophie Ellis-Bextor

'I should say the most important quality I possess is my ability to get right to the hearts of children and enable them to see things in the right way.

'I don't really know how I get to the hearts of children. I only know that I love them, I want them to grow up into good, decent grown-ups. I want them to be kind and loving and generous.

'That sounds, of course, very pious, but it isn't pious, it isn't pious at all. It's simply and solely what every single mother really in her heart of hearts wants for her own child, and I just happen to want it for all children.'

Enid Blyton, 1963

'I'm very critical of my own (Catholic) church in its attitude towards birth control. I think it's indefensible. You can't tell modern women to have as many children as biology will allow them to do, because they won't do it, and what you actually then get is a kind of hypocrisy where the Church goes on asserting its opposition to birth control, and 90% of Catholic women in developed countries use it. On the other hand, I do agree with them about abortion. I think abortion is very serious and it should not be treated casually, as it is being ... To actually not go into the issues but simply facilitate an abortion for a young woman, or whatever it may be, I don't think that's acceptable.'

Baroness Shirley Williams

'[My daughter] changed my perspective drastically. I'm much calmer now than I was before I had Annie. She has made me realise the truth of something that I'd heard all my life but never really understood, which is what's important is the moment. Moment-to-moment living. And that life is right now. It's not tomorrow, it's not six months from now. Because she's such a spontaneous moment-to-moment little being herself.

'I've always been very much of a perfectionist and rather single-minded. They're not two easy traits for someone else to live with. But I think that Annie has mellowed me a lot.'

**Actress Glenn Close, a year after
the birth of daughter Annie**

Although Doris Lessing had three children in two marriages,
she left her eldest two – John and Jean – with their father in
South Africa when she moved to London in 1949. She brought
three-year-old Peter with her and raised him as a single mum.

'It's much easier to bring up girls than boys, my guess is.

   'I have brought up a son without a father, which I would advise no woman should do because it was awful and very bad for him. But a girl is different.

   'Your daughter's your daughter for all of her life. Your son is your son till he gets him a wife. I've just seen this happening. It is horrifying. This betrayed woman, very nice woman, her son has got himself a girlfriend and has moved in. [She says] "I'm betrayed, I hate her, I can't forgive." I say, "For God's sake! But this is life, is it not?" This is a very useful little adage.'

Doris Lessing

*Bette Davis had one natural daughter, Barbara, and adopted
two more children, Margot and Michael. Margot was
institutionalised after being diagnosed with severe brain
damage at the age of three. In 1979, the actress was less than
happy when asked about her 'adopted' children.*

'They're all mine. I am so tired of the adoption thing.
They came out of hospital when they were five days old
and if I wasn't famous they would probably never have to
know they were adopted. I have two daughters and a son,
that's all.'

Bette Davis

————◆•◆————

'I used to read [my children] my stories after I had written
them, and if there was anything in the stories they didn't
like, I knew that story had to be altered, or if there was
anything frightening, out it came. I used them as my
stooges and I think probably thousands of children benefit
from the fact that my children were such good critics.'

Enid Blyton

'One worrying statistic is that 50 per cent of children, by the time they are fifteen, will have parents that have separated and of those relationships that break up 80 per cent were just living together. So the only thing I would say about it is that marriage makes people try harder therefore from a children's point of view – and I think children are so important – I think marriage is a good thing.'

Jilly Cooper, 2011

Baroness Tanni Grey-Thompson is one of the UK's most successful Paralympians, with sixteen medals including eleven golds. Married to research chemist Dr Ian Thompson, she was shocked to find some people couldn't accept the idea of her becoming a mum.

'I had people stop me in the street and say to me when I was about seven months pregnant, "You're pregnant. How did you get pregnant?" And this was a complete stranger.

'I was quite rude back. I have to say, I was slightly psychotic and hormonal. I did shout back to her that I had sex with my husband, and sorry about that, and she said, "That's disgusting. People like you shouldn't have sex," and walked off.

'There's this presumption that if you're disabled, then obviously you're not having sex with anybody. You wouldn't possibly do it. And there's also this presumption that you might not be married. People have quite unusual opinions on the starting level of what someone can achieve with a disability.'

Baroness Tanni Grey-Thompson, 2012

Barbara Walters is a pioneering broadcaster who made history in 1976 when she became the first female co-anchor on a major network's evening news, and landed a salary of $1 million. At the time she was a single mum to daughter Jacqueline and, in 1979, she told Woman's Hour *it was time to slow down.*

'[Life as a news journalist] sounds if not glamorous, awfully exciting and it is but I find now, and perhaps it's a different stage of my life, that I want to travel much less, that I want to work much less, that I want to get out of the day-to-day covering of news.

'I have a little girl who's ten and I hear a great deal about the quality of time, that that's much more important than the quantity of time we spend with the child and it's true. But you've got to have that time. You've got to have those minutes or hours with your child to have any quality. She's growing up and I want to be with her more. I want to have more of a private life.'

Barbara Walters

'I had no particular desire to be married. I think the only reason to get married is to have children. I felt that with two or three or four of my younger [siblings], I'd taken care of them so it was an experience I'd had already and I felt I was too selfish to be a mother. I think I was probably wrong. Now I wonder what it would be like but my concentration was so total in what I was doing that it never bothered me.'

Katharine Hepburn, aged 84, in 1991

'I think it's a mistake to be only a wife and mother. It's not fair on your husband and it's not fair on your children. What they want is a person, not a role player.'

Fay Weldon, 1974

'It should be a world centred on children. The only thing we are really here for, as human beings, is to reproduce ourselves. I don't mean that everyone has to have children, I don't mean that at all, but that raising children, having children and raising children should be the central and primary task of every human society, because it's the only important thing we do.

'But nowadays if you live in a city and you have a job and you have a child, you're living in hell. You're living in as close to hell as there is. It's horribly hard. It's almost impossible. All of life should be centred on making the raising of children a healthy, happy, sensible, pleasant activity.'

Author Marilyn French

'I remember my kids said their lizard died and I said, "Yeah, yeah, here's my credit card. Go get him cremated." So I thought, I can't miss any more. These days, although nothing is 100 per cent, but sometimes when I'm talking to them a bit of my brain has that overview and is saying, "Ruby, your fingers are on the keyboard!" People can tell when you're not paying attention. They don't know you're thinking "Where did I leave my keys?" but they know you're not home. But you focus on those kids and you really listen and boy, do they open up. That's the trick to teenagers. You don't have to see them all day, just be present when they're there, hold your anchor and don't get caught in the "It's your fault", "It's my fault." If you can hold your ground and really be present, they'll open their hearts.'

Ruby Wax, 2017

'It's very hard to work at a career when you have small children because you have to leave them with other people and I tried to combine a career in television at one point and still be home when the school bus got there. It was kind of touch and go sometimes but I did manage.'

Actress and politician Shirley Temple Black, 1976

'It's difficult for anyone who has a big job because you're always juggling. If you love your children, if you enjoy being with them, I defy anyone to say that's an easy thing to do. But women have been doing that since time immemorial and doing it well. And, I think, we'll still do it well.'

Baroness Scotland on working as a government minister while raising two small children

---

Shortly after giving birth to daughter Annie, Glenn Close was back on set to film Dangerous Liaisons *with John Malkovich and Michelle Pfeiffer.*

'I was so tired I couldn't remember my lines. And that's never happened to me. And it was just because Annie at the time didn't have any hours. She didn't sleep through the night.

'So I would come home after working sometimes ten, twelve hours, and I tried to stay up with her as much as possible until I would literally almost collapse. And then crawl into bed and get up early in the morning. And so I was really burning the candle at both ends. And it almost did me in physically. But it didn't matter. Everything was worthwhile.'

Glenn Close, 1989

'When Shirley was put into my arms, when I looked at my red-headed little daughter, I experienced a much greater satisfaction than when returning officers said I was a Member of Parliament.

'Let me quickly say that I had responded to my maternal instincts and satisfied them, but if I hadn't been able to use my mind, I think I would have been so frustrated that I would not have been an extremely pleasant wife and mother.'

**Doctor and Labour MP Edith Summerskill,
who became an MP in 1938**

'You've got to know what you want from technology and you've got to say not, "Oh gosh I have got to have my ten week scan because they say I have to have it." You have to say to yourself "Well do I really want to meet my child on television or do I want to be able to say this is my pregnancy, I'll handle it?"'

Germaine Greer, 1999

'They say breast is best and I have been feeding her myself and it's awfully difficult to do that over a distance of five miles if I leave her at home. I may have achieved a new voluptuousness since having her but I'm not so voluptuous I can reach over five miles! So she has to come at what they call in the zoo, "feeding time". That is very nice for me because it means I have a reason why I have to see her at lunchtime and at 6 o'clock in the evening.

'There is another reason too which is that I adore her company and if it came to a point that work prevented me seeing the baby, work would have to go.'

**TV star Esther Rantzen explains why
daughter Emily, then a few months
old, came to work with her in 1978**

'The most one can hope for is that when they grow up and leave home, they will keep in touch with each other and, if it isn't too much to hope for, love each other.'

**Writer Shirley Conran on her hopes
for her two sons**

'I always believed that it was the quality of time, not the quantity, that mattered. My father had very little time for the children but we all loved him and we looked forward to him being with us, so the time that I do spend both with my husband and my child is well spent.'

Benazir Bhutto speaking in 1989, five months after the birth of her son and just three months after being elected Prime Minister of Pakistan

------◆------

Between 1989 and 2010, Aung San Suu Kyi spent a total of fifteen years under house arrest in Burma, after the military junta refused to recognise her as the elected president. During that time she was unable to see her two sons by English husband Michael Aris, who stayed with him in the UK. She spoke to Woman's Hour *by telephone in 1995 about missing their adolescence.*

'It's not much of a sacrifice compared to what other people have had to go through. My colleagues in prison do not have the comfort of knowing their children are safe and yet they went on because they believed in what they were doing.

'Of course if one thinks of one's family, one missed them but if you have to work as hard as we have to do in Burma, you really don't have much time to indulge your own personal emotions.'

Aung San Suu Kyi

'My personal view is that the one really important aspect of giving birth to children – seeking treatment if you're infertile and so on – is that having a child should not be trivialised. This means that in cases where somebody seeks genetic intervention to produce a child who they think will be a violinist or a ballet dancer, or have blue eyes, this is, it seems to me, a trivialisation of the relationship between child and parent which in my view should be essentially loving of the child, whatever he or she is like.'

Dame Mary Warnock, eminent philosopher who, in 1982, chaired a committee to come up with a legal framework for the practice of in vitro fertilisation

'I graduated from college, I was married three days later and had twin daughters two years after that. And because they were premature and they had to be fed every three hours, and it took them an hour to feed, I just went pretty crazy. I watched television and just kind of sat there.'

Madeleine Albright, who became the first female Secretary of State in the US in 1997

Sharon and Ozzy Osbourne have three children, Aimee, Jack and Kelly. When they chose to document their daily lives in the TV show The Osbournes *Aimee refused to take part. Afterwards Jack and Kelly both battled drug addictions.*

'I don't honestly think, to be truthful, that my kids went off the rails just because the cameras were there. They would have gone anyway.

'[I partly blame myself] because I'm their mum. You're meant to know your kids better than anyone in your life and I didn't see it happening.'

Sharon Osbourne, 2004

'I had my first baby when I was 25 and I was feeling quite surprised, excited but overwhelmed with the idea and my second album had just come out. My mum said to me, "The good thing about being a young mum is that you have permission to be selfish." That really gave me a lot of freedom because that's what I had really been concerned about – how can I still do things for me now that the centre of my world is my baby? It spurred me on to still be ambitious for myself and think that it was alright that I wanted to keep working.'

Sophie Ellis-Bextor

'Before he left home my eldest son said to me, "I think you've done a good job of bringing me up." I was stunned. I stopped peeling the potatoes or whatever I was doing and said "Why? Tell me quick." And he said: "Well I've got this terrible lisp, this speech impediment, and I'm very small, almost a dwarf, and I'm practically blind – and you don't care."'

Shirley Conran, 1979

LOVE AND
RELATIONSHIPS

From whirlwind love affairs and long happy marriages, to abusive partners and heartbreak, every kind of relationship has been discussed over the 70 years of the programme.

'Most men had more self-preservation than to think marriage to me was a going concern.'

Germaine Greer, 1999

Actress Felicity Kendal married Michael Rudman in 1983 and divorced him in 1990. But after an affair with Tom Stoppard she was reunited with Michael and the pair are still in a long-term relationship.

'We got together and were very happy together but the marriage didn't work for all sorts of reasons, so we divorced. But it didn't work, and it was a really bad divorce in that it didn't take. We still saw each other all the time and eventually got back together again.

   'I'm not saying we wouldn't marry but not at the moment because it's more fun not being married. We tried the married bit and it didn't work very well so he's my toyboy now. It's a good arrangement. It's more exciting and we can still terrify each other. There's something about "Well where were you today?" which seems to work for us.'

Felicity Kendal, 2016

'The lesson is there as it always has been, that if you fall in love with somebody else's husband, if you play away from home, then you're running risks with your heart and your general sense of wellbeing, your emotional wellbeing. It can lead you into false judgments. It can lead you into thinking somebody is much better than they are. It can lead you into secrets.'

Edwina Currie, in 2002, reflecting on her famous affair with John Major

'Words are everything. People fall in love because of words in romantic comedy. They break up because of words. Everything is made right because of the right words.'

Nora Ephron

'The generation of the Sixties, in whom I have to include myself, believed that sex was a panacea. We were forbidden to have sex, therefore we thought that when we were allowed to have sex, it would solve all our problems.

'What we discovered was what men had always known. There is a difference between lust and love, there is a difference between lust and friendship. We now could go out and have all the sex we wanted and we discovered that sex indiscriminately used becomes a kind of servitude and bondage.'

Author Erica Jong, 2014

In 1969, Jilly Cooper wrote How to Stay Married, *having wed husband Leo seven years earlier. In 2011, she returned to* Woman's Hour *to revisit her own advice, including the assertion that if you refuse sex for more than two nights you 'deserve to be cheated on'.*

'Sex, if it's going along well, is so lovely and it does cheer people up and it's a wonderful thing. It brings people together and makes people happy so to go on saying no all the time is a bit depressing. When one was young sex was lovely and if you don't get out of the habit of lots of sex then you enjoy it and it's fun.'

Jilly Cooper, 2011

Author and Chef Prue Leith was widowed in 2002. In October 2016 she wed her second husband John Playfair.

'He is my toyboy. I'm 76 and he's 70. We've been together for five years and I don't know why we got married but we both decided it was the right moment. I suppose it's something to do with commitment, the idea that yes, we are prepared to push each other around in our zimmer frames and bath chairs and we want to spend the rest of our lives together.'

Prue Leith

'Without a doubt the reason that my first marriage ended in divorce, and the divorce I didn't in any way myself want, was that there just wasn't enough time together, and understandably, therefore, my husband looked elsewhere for people who would listen very carefully to what he had and who were totally committed to his welfare, his comfort, which I can't pretend I was because my job didn't allow it.'

Baroness Shirley Williams, 2004

'Have you been reading, by any chance, *Bridget Jones's Diary*, or seeing it? I saw it on the box the other night. It's quite a revelation, and it was written as a joke, apparently. Other people have done it better. Jane Austen did it better, but here we have girls looking for Mr Right, which as far as I can see is what they're doing. They want Mr Right. So not much [has changed].

'But certain things have changed, and that is a lot of women are not having children. In other words, they have choice, which they never had before, which I think is a real revolution. I think the Pill is the real revolution of our times.'

Doris Lessing, 2008

'One evening in the Café Royal, instead of going to the Open Room where all you needed to be able to afford was a cup of coffee and a sandwich, Nye had ordered a table for two, everything was in order, and then at a certain point he says to me, "Now, we've got to get married."'

'Let's be fair, there's a great deal of hypocrisy these days. Nye and I were living together. Neither of us wanted marriage in the sense that we wanted to be free, whatever happened. We were dedicated Socialists. But Nye, with his way of doing business, said to me on this evening, "Now, we've got to get married. We can't go on living in sin."'

'Young ones don't talk that language nowadays, and he did it, of course, with a smile and a chuckle. He said, "They won't like it in Wales in my non-conformist constituency, but I think I can survive, but in North Lanark, if gossip gets around, it will destroy you." And I was standing as an ILP candidate, and I said, "Alright, Nye, we'll get married."'

Labour peer Jennie Lee, Baroness Lee of Asherbridge on the proposal from her future husband, Aneurin Bevan, 1980

'We like our romantic couples to look a little bit alike. Then the truth is when you look at the world, people often look just a little bit like they go with their spouse. People tend to be kind of salt and pepper shakers in some way. The number of roly-poly people who marry one another, and the number of very skinny people, and the tall people.

'I always feel it's so tragic when I see a really tall man with a really short woman, because it seems as if they each could have made someone just like themselves very happy.'

Nora Ephron, 1999

—◆—

Author Doris Lessing moved to London in 1949 with her young son Peter after divorcing second husband Gottfried Lessing.

'I did [miss having a man] for a time, but I also lived with people without ever saying so or writing about it, quietly. I didn't have a long live-in lover, which I should have had, but it would have suited me very well. Then it got too late. You know that very well, there's a time where it gets a bit late to say, "Where is my bloke?" Well, you've had that one, haven't you, mate?'

Doris Lessing

'I think I was very lucky to marry a man who had been married before so when I got panicky he would say, "Don't worry darling, marriage is like this. Don't pack your bags." I married a very nice man so I was lucky.'

Jilly Cooper on husband Leo

'I'm a very romantic person. I definitely was one of those people who was just going to keep on getting married until I finally got it right, and if this one hadn't worked out I'd be married to the next one and trying with the next one. It only took three tries to get it right.'

Nora Ephron on her third marriage to screenwriter Nicholas Pileggi

'I think it's lovely to dress up to please somebody. I don't do it very often but my mother always looked very pretty when my father came home. It's lovely for a husband to come home to a fragrant scented wife, but it's very hard on the wife and she can't do it all the time.'

Jilly Cooper, 2011

Katharine Hepburn had a thirty-year affair with screen idol Spencer Tracy, even though he remained married to wife Louise throughout. In the 1960s, when he fell ill, the actress took a five-year break to look after him.

'The last five or six years that I was with Spencer, we lived in the same house. He wasn't all that well and I thought I should be in the same house with him and I was. I think marriage is difficult from that point of view if the two people are very close together all the time and they cease to interest each other. But if they don't cease to interest each other, then I would say it's a very lasting friendship.'

Katharine Hepburn, 1991

'The way to work a career and marriage ... number one, marriage is most important I think, at least for me, and having children was most important. That's really the role of women. But if a woman has the opportunity and the initiative to work also, I certainly think she should have full rights and opportunities and equal pay.'

Shirley Temple Black, 1976

Punk legends Vivienne Westwood and Malcolm McLaren were partners for over a decade and had a son, Joe, in 1967.

'It was not a happy relationship. I stayed with Malcolm out of a great loyalty to him because I knew that he really needed me, whatever he was doing. It was like fencing with somebody. He could not leave the house in the morning without wounding me in some way. Then he could do something.'

Dame Vivienne Westwood, 2014

'I always wanted as a child to like Aesop's fables. My teachers were constantly reading them to me. But I was very disappointed in them. They never rang true. The little morals at the end seemed false. So I sort of thought, well, what would Mrs Aesop have thought of this? He's so clichéd, Aesop, that I could imagine her being bored to death by his fables all the time.'

Poet Carol Ann Duffy, 1999

'I don't think we really took to each other at first sight. He told me he didn't like my singing – he thought it was "corny".'

Dame Vera Lynn recalls meeting future husband Harry Lewis. Their subsequent marriage lasted 58 years

Despite being a ground-breaking female politician and an advocate of women's rights, Benazir Bhutto agreed to an arranged marriage in 1987, to Asif Ali Zadari.

'For many years [arranged marriage] was an idea I found hard to accept, but once I had made my mind up for religious reasons that it was a step that had to be taken, that put an end to soul-searching.'

Benazir Bhutto, 1989

———◆◆◆———

'It's easy for people to say "Why didn't you leave him" but you can't leave a man when you have six children under eight. You can't just go. I married for life. I didn't marry to leave when the going got tough.'

Elisabeth Maxwell, wife of media mogul Robert, in 1994 after claiming in her biography that he bullied her and their six children

'I remember finding some bits of rubber in the bottom of my mum's wardrobe and saying, "What's that Mum?" and she got very embarrassed about it, so they did know what to do. But it wasn't anywhere near as convenient or as much of a contribution to freedom as the Pill in the 1960s.'

Edwina Currie, 2016

'In my experience men are desperate to get married. They're desperate to make you settle down. They want to marry you from the moment you meet them and then you have to dump them.'

Julie Burchill, 1999

'The fact of the matter is there are a lot of women out there who complain about men and their relationships, but they're not willing to do anything about it. Love is not a reason to stay with somebody if they're not treating you right. And I think it's more important when there are children involved.

'I don't think it should be about yourself. I think that's very selfish. I think we've spent a lot of time saying "men this, men that". But the men who are out there are the way they are. They are never going to change unless we, as women, stop putting up with it.'

Ms Dynamite, 2002

In 1995, President Bill Clinton had a brief sexual dalliance with 22-year-old intern Monica Lewinsky. In 2003, the former First Lady reflected on her decision to stand by him in the wake of the ensuing scandal.

'When you love someone you accept that there is no perfect person, as far as I am aware. Love and marriage happens between two imperfect people, and they have strengths and weaknesses, attributes and detriments.'

Hillary Clinton, 2003

Jilly Cooper's fifty-year marriage to husband Leo survived the revelation of his six-year affair with another woman. In 2011 Jilly spoke about how to deal with an unfaithful partner.

'In every marriage, when you love somebody very much, you worry about them being in love with somebody else and you think that perhaps they might meet some pretty woman at a party. You try and keep your trap shut for a bit but obviously when you are confronted by something you have to act up and say, "Please stop this."'

Jilly Cooper

After falling in love at the age of 71, with future husband John Playfair, Prue Leith admitted to 'butterflies in her stomach'.

'Why would it be any different? If you really want somebody to ring you up and they're not ringing you up it's exactly like when you're sixteen. You think "What have I done? What's happened? Is he going to ring?" All that goes on. I sat there thinking: "How do I write this text so it doesn't sound pushy but it still reminds him I'm here?"'

Prue Leith

'You don't find the good men until you have learned to be alone. Yes, there are good men to be had, but you won't find them if you go after them with this desperate need. I think you find the good men when you are centred enough, when you have enough self-esteem, when you like digging your garden and you like puttering around your house, and you'd rather be alone than be with a dirty, rotten rat.

'It basically has to do with learning good self-esteem and learning how to like your own company. I feel so happy in my own company now that if I can't be with somebody who genuinely gives me joy, I'd much rather be alone.'

Erica Jong

'I did go into a chat room just to see what it was. I tried for weeks to get into the Over 40 Room on America Online. It was always crammed full of people. Finally I got into it and it seemed to me to have a lot of fourteen-year-old boys in it pretending to be over 40. No one could spell, so I left because I do not see myself living happily ever after with anyone who can't spell.'

Nora Ephron on the perils of internet dating

HEALTH AND LIFESTYLE

Between work, family and the stresses of modern life, health and relaxation often takes a back seat for today's busy women. But here's how some of the Woman's Hour *guests make the most of their lifestyle and, in some cases, deal with the tough health issues they have faced along the way.*

'I adored being rich. I remember someone yelled out one night "Mr Astor's a millionaire, ain't he?" And poor Mr Astor looked very embarrassed but I looked up and said: "I pray God he is, that's one of the reasons I married him."'

Britain's first female MP, Nancy Astor, 1956

———◆◆◆———

'Well things are really good for me now, I'm very healthy, I'm strong, I love my work, I love my life, I really love my friends and my family, I think of everything that has happened in the past and I think, "Oh, who knows?", but I'm going through a very, very, very, good bit.

'The hep C was a shock. I had treatment and it's really fine now. I'm perfectly alright. The breast cancer was not really bad – it was pre-cancer so they found it very early, and they took it out. I didn't even have to have chemo … I have a couple of friends who are going through that at the moment and they're having the most awful time. All I can say is the most important thing is to have those checks.'

Marianne Faithfull, 2013

'I like the simple life, frankly, so I am just myself all the time, except when I'm performing in a play or a motion picture, then I take on the character. I don't drink and I don't smoke and I have found that my way for really living is to live simply and correctly. I enjoy it.'

Screen legend Ginger Rogers, 1969

'I've just spent a wonderful three months sitting back and relaxing in the South of France. I'm relaxing much more. I think that I could never, ever retire. I enjoy life too much. There are too many things I want to do – travelling, writing, acting, seeing people, going places. I have the same energy and vitality and ambition – well maybe not ambition – that I had thirty years ago, it hasn't changed. I can still get up and I can still do 150 sit ups, probably because I've always done 150 sit ups. If I'd stopped, I couldn't.'

Joan Collins, aged 63, in 1986

Film actress Angelina Jolie underwent a double mastectomy after discovering she had inherited the defective BRCA1 gene, giving her an 87 per cent chance of developing breast cancer. Two years later she had her ovaries removed to prevent the ovarian cancer which had killed her mother and grandmother.

'It wasn't really a decision. I thought that I had gained information that I wish my mother had known. I wish she'd had the option, I wish she'd had the surgery, in fact. It might have given her more years with my family.

'So I wanted to speak with other women and talk about options and it is simply that, an option. I don't encourage every woman to make the decision I made but I think it's important we all share anything we learn.'

Angelina Jolie, 2016

'I went through a period, of about three hours, of just crying and shaking and then after the three hours was over something else swept in and I can describe it best as a feeling of the warrior. I was all of a sudden the warrior and I had something to fight against.

'All my life I've been a warrior with just little skirmishes, little kind of border fights, and this was a big fight and so all of a sudden the warrior in me rose up and said, "Now we have a big thing to deal with," and so I mobilised my forces, emotional and physical.'

Carly Simon, on being diagnosed with breast cancer

'You feel as if you've been in some kind of a battle, and you have your battle scars. Losing a breast for a woman is traumatic.

'When you're in the public eye you have people kind of looking at you saying, "Oh, I wonder which one it is?". But you can adapt to almost anything. I think having two breasts was always overrated anyway.'

Carly Simon on being treated for breast cancer and having a mastectomy, 1999

Former child star Shirley Temple Black had a radical
mastectomy in 1972, after being diagnosed with breast cancer.
She immediately announced the results of the operation on TV
and radio and became one of the first women to openly talk
about her breast cancer. In 1976, she explained her decision to
Woman's Hour.

'It was difficult in a way because I didn't want to do
anything that would embarrass my children or my
husband. So right after the surgery, I called my husband
and children into my hospital room and said, would you
object if I make this operation known because I have a
reason for doing it? I want to let other women know,
my sisters in the world, that they should have medical
check-ups and they should make sure that this is caught
in time.

'I got 50,000 letters from women all over the world,
a great many from the United Kingdom, and I feel that
perhaps I have saved a life, maybe more than one. In fact
I'm sure it's more than one.'

Actress and politician Shirley Temple Black

'My mother had a drink problem; she was a bender drinker. I think my number was marked. It was extraordinary, having gone through a childhood where my mother's drinking was very much part of it. I was conscious of this and it was very upsetting. There was a certain sort of inevitability in it rather than a choice.'

Anne Robinson reflects on her own battle with alcohol addiction in 2001

━━◆━━

'Eating is a worse addiction than drinking. It's a terrible addiction to have and it never ends. I just don't think you ever get over it.'

Sharon Osbourne on her weight battles, 2004

'One thing that does concern me is that so many young women now think they have to do university, then twenty years in a career and then they want a family and that can be a route to a lot of misery. If you think you might like a family it's not a bad idea to have that in your head early on and have healthy kids without having to have IVF or all the rest of it. A member of my family had been exactly through that and it's a miserable and unhappy business.'

Edwina Currie, 2016

'I went to the university doctor to ask for contraception and I was given a huge, raging, furious denunciation of the morals of my generation. The fact that I was an unmarried virgin (let's say that for the moment) shocked him and he thought it was disgusting of me.'

Novelist Marina Warner reflecting on her attempts to get the Pill at Oxford University in the 1960s

'I think it's a very mixed time for women. Some of the difficulties are having things in extremis, that everything has to be awesome or absolutely terrible and there's not enough complexity in our emotional lives. I think a way to have resilience is not only through friendship and community but also to dare to know what you feel, to dare to accept your vulnerabilities and your difficulties. Allowing those vulnerabilities to exist inside of you gives you enormous strength.'

Psychotherapist Susie Orbach, 2016

'When I went to university there was a notice on the wall saying the college doctor would give a talk on relationships to the first-years and I thought "I come from Liverpool and I've been to America so I don't need to do anything like that." But there was an almighty row afterwards because he was talking about contraception to unmarried virgins in Oxford. I thought he did something responsible but there was all sorts of fuss about it and it was thought a very naughty thing to do but by golly, we'd been listening and we took advantage.'

Edwina Currie, 2016

SELF IMAGE

Whatever our age, looking good and feeling good are important to our self-confidence. But the debate rages over how women are portrayed in the mainstream media, whether the expectations of women are realistic when it comes to appearance and the image of the role models presented to younger women today. Here some Woman's Hour *guests share some thoughts on everything from shoes to body-image*

In 1999, actress and chat show host Oprah Winfrey was chosen to be on the cover of Vogue, *but lost weight for the shoot. A year later she told* Woman's Hour *why she decided to slim down to become a cover girl.*

'I grew up "coloured", ugly, skinny, looking like buckwheat. Just the idea that that little girl could grow up and be on the cover of *Vogue* so thrilled me. Yes, I had to lose weight but you would too if Anna Wintour came to you and said, "Do you want to be on the cover of *Vogue*?"

'As it is I'm the largest person who has ever been on the cover. I was not as skinny as anything. I weighed 150 pounds [10st 10lb] that day and was between a size 8 and a 10 [US] and there were still dresses I couldn't fit myself into. To *Vogue* I was a large-sized girl.

'The truth is that people lose weight for their children's bat mitzvahs. They lose weight for their son's wedding, they lose weight when they are going to their family reunion or a high school reunion, because you feel better and you fit the clothes.

'I didn't sell out, I did it because "Do you want to be on the cover of *Vogue*? Then this is how you have to look." Otherwise don't. It didn't define my life.

'I didn't think I could hold that weight. I've gained 20 pounds since then and today I've started working out again. I have to work so hard. I've been that weight before but in order for me to stay a size 8 I have to work out at least an hour a day and eat almost nothing and I'm not prepared to do that. What kind of life is that without a French fry *ever*?'

Oprah Winfrey on her famous
***Vogue* cover of 1999**

'There are definitely more important things than shoes but having said that I like shoes and I have often wondered why women are so obsessed with this particular item of clothing. I think it's undeniable that shoes come first as the most mythologised, fetishised item, I'd say. They turn up so often in stories and fairy tales, so what is the power and myth of the shoe?

'I'm not a pumps girl. I'm not a sensible flats girl. I do own some flat boots because there comes a point when it becomes a bit ridiculous. You do need to be able to walk the dog and I do walk the dog, and I don't do that in stilettoes, but I love a heel, I'm short – I'm only 5ft 4in – but people are often surprised how short I am because I wear heels and they assume I'm a nice willowy 5ft 9in, which shows you what high shoes I wear.'

**Author JK Rowling reflects on
the nation's shoe fetish, 2014**

Dame Helen Mirren has famously stripped off many a time on screen. In 1979, she revealed her feelings about nudity when she's off camera.

'When I was younger, I was an intensely physically shy person but also a dreamer and a fantasist so I guess the two things went hand in hand, contradictorily hand in hand. But I'm quite happy to have my clothes off on a nudist beach. I quite like nudism actually, I find the liberation and the equality of being on a beach where young and old and beautiful and ugly and fat and thin people are just naked together ... somehow taking clothes away opens up people's quality in a way that is quite extraordinary. And it's a lovely feeling – being out in the open air and the sea and all the rest of it.'

Helen Mirren

*Actress Kate Winslet was made a household name by the
1997 epic* Titanic *and three years later starred in the drama*
Holy Smoke. *The Jane Campion film included a controversial
scene where a naked Kate urinates on screen.*

'I would just never do anything I felt was unnecessary or
gratuitous and believe me, when shooting nude scenes
or love scenes, I am pretty firm about how they're being
shot. I want to see everything after we've shot it, not
because I'm concerned about that bit that I don't like and
this bit that I don't like but because if there's something
that I feel is too much and isn't actually telling the story,
then I'll just say, "Look, I'm not happy with that, let's try
something different."

'For me, I will always do things that I feel are important
to the character's journey and with *Holy Smoke*, all the
nudity in that I felt was so crucial. The scene that you
just mentioned, the urinating scene, Ruth is actually going
slightly mad then and is at her most vulnerable in the
whole story so to me, whilst I kept putting it off in my
brain thinking that scene will just go away and I'll never
actually have to shoot it, when I came to shoot it I was
really given confidence by the fact that it was there for
such good reason.'

Kate Winslet, 1999

'I have never felt that fashion was for being any special age or for doing any special thing in. I think that [Coco] Chanel understood this very well. I remember seeing her just a couple of years before she died, she must have been 80. She was sitting in the Ritz in Paris and she was wearing a cream suit with sort of chocolate velvet brown braid round the edge and a brown velvet hat, looking absolutely wonderful, incredible for 80-something, and yet that suit could equally have been worn by a girl of fourteen who in her way would look marvellous. I don't really believe clothes are designed for special ages. I have never thought so.'

Mary Quant, 1971

'I think my clothes are extremely heroic. I like to make women feel and look important. I do believe that people need power as much as they need love.'

Vivienne Westwood, 2004

'Corsets are pretty amazing because they do change your posture. They do make you sit in a different way, and I do have really large breasts so the corsets kind of suit me. You know those women that used to be on the front of a ship in the 18th century? I always think that I look like one of those women when I'm wearing one of the corsets.'

Tracey Emin on Vivienne Westwood, 2004

———◆———

'I'd always loved clothes. I think it stems mainly from my mum and my sisters because Mum had always made my clothes so I got into dressmaking from Mum.

'I still [make clothes] I love it, it's my hobby. I can't cook, but I'm a good little sewer!'

Twiggy, 1975

'[The Queen Mother] always surprised me with the clothes she wore because no matter what the weather was, she'd always come out in those flimsy clothes and I'd think she must be cold. Perhaps she had some thermals underneath!'

Dame Vera Lynn, 2002

———◆◦◆———

'There was a time when the commentators went through a period of saying, "She always wears pearls." Well I thought, "Why shouldn't I wear pearls?" There is a very strong reason why I wear them. They were given to me by my husband when the children were born. And I shall go on wearing them.'

Margaret Thatcher, 1976

'You do play around with women's proportions and sometimes, you know, I love to put women on a pedestal and give them these high-heeled shoes. And that's why I invented the platforms, and that's why they took the particular form that they did, because I wanted it to be like a pedestal.'

Vivienne Westwood

'I don't think we should mistake supermodels for real life; it is a gorgeous freakish sideshow ... this isn't the way that women should look. Men have thought it up. It's what twelve [men] in Paris, New York and London think we should look like.'

Julie Burchill, 1999

'If every woman in the [music] industry said, "I'm not prepared to do that, I want people to judge me on my talent rather than my body" there wouldn't be any women flaunting their bit about. And what would people do? Not play women's songs because they don't show their body? I don't think that would ever happen.

'There is pressure there but as women we make it worse for ourselves.'

Mercury Prize-winner Ms Dynamite, 2002

'Despite the various things I've said or written there seems to be the impulse to describe me as this kind of perfect creature who is whipping up cakes at all hours, reading stories to my children, spraying myself with expensive French scent.'

Nigella Lawson, 2000

'I'd always had a weight problem my entire life. I'm one of those girls that put on 50 pounds, lost 50 pounds, then put on 65, then lost the 65 pounds and put on 100! My entire life I have been yo-yoing. About five years ago my back was really hurting and my feet. When I'd go up the stairs [my son] Jack would have to be behind me, lifting my bum up the stairs because I couldn't make these stairs, they were killing me.

'I've tried every diet in the world and I couldn't stop eating so I had an operation on my stomach to make my stomach smaller. I lost 125 pounds and then I had all this hanging skin everywhere so I decided, when I lost all the weight, now I can get rid of it all and have nice boobs and things.'

X Factor judge Sharon Osbourne on her battle with weight and her plastic surgery

'The name Twiggy came out of my being so thin and [boyfriend and manager Justin de Villeneuve] and his brother called me it as a nickname when I was still at school. It started out as "Sticks" actually and then it turned into Twiggy.'

Twiggy, 1975

———◆◆◆———

'I often think I'm a designer for fashion because I get bored with clothes terribly quickly, and I'm never satisfied with whatever it is and I'm always experimenting with something new, and I find that fashion seems to evolve quite logically. A kind of fed-upness with the last thing, I mean, the experimenting again, and the new things grow out of whatever one's been doing before or just, you know, an idea that's still bugging one and exciting one that one hasn't yet quite got right.'

Mary Quant

When JK Rowling shot to fame, on publication of Harry Potter and the Philosopher's Stone *in 1997, she was not prepared for the onslaught of comment on her appearance. When she was guest editor on* Woman's Hour *she revealed how she dealt with the negative press.*

'I found it difficult when I first became well known to read criticism of how I looked, how messy my hair was and how generally unkempt I looked. But you can go one of two ways. You can be the person who I would admire who says, "I don't care. I will continue to not bother to brush my hair," or you can be a weak-willed person like me and think "I'd better get my act together." So I did tidy myself up a bit.

'But I do resent the time it takes to get my act together and smarten up to be on TV. It must be so nice to be a man and think "Which of my three suits shall I wear today?"'

JK Rowling, 2014

'It was a period when there were a lot of dolly birds in short skirts with wonderful bouffant hair and false eyelashes. They created this Barbara Goode character who adored her husband and was attracted to him sexually, had no children or responsibilities and was there for him whatever rubbish ideas he had and she didn't mind what she looked like. I think that was what was attractive to men in the sense that it wasn't a threat. If she'd been in a bikini with a six-pack it might have been rather threatening and attractive – but only for a Saturday evening.'

Felicity Kendal on why men fell in love with her character in *The Good Life*

FRIENDSHIP

As the cliché goes, 'You can choose your friends but you can't choose your family.' They feature in your fondest memories, are always around when you need a good laugh, or a shoulder to cry on and, in the trials and tribulations of life, it is often your closest friends that get you through.

Over the years, our guests have covered every aspect of female friendship on the show – from the unbreakable bond of a true friend, to betrayal, the falseness of Facebook friendships and even 'friendship culling'.

'Friendship is one of the essential things like food and drink and work and children. It's one of the basics of life.

'Life is hard. You need help to get through it, and friendship is one of the things that helps you get through it.'

Marilyn French, author of *The Women's Room*

'I think for women particularly, your friendships really get you through the good and the bad times … People write about love stories but I think when you find your best friend it can feel like that. It's the person who is there consistently throughout your life no matter what, when – particularly in the early part of your life – men come and go, life changes, you move around, you change jobs, you have all these different experiences but this one person can see you through all of that.'

Writer and TV presenter Dawn O'Porter, 2014

Broadcaster Vanessa Feltz divorced the father of her children, Michael Kurer, in 2000, after he left her for another woman. But her ex-husband wasn't the only one to let her down.

'Lots of my friends, the vast majority of them, seemed to disappear in the ether and it was a very strange and unpleasant and heart-breaking time in so many ways. I had prided myself on having real friends, people I'd really grown up with and I'd know at kindergarten and who lived round the corner when I was growing up, so I hadn't found fame and fortune and notoriety and ditched all my real friends and gone off with Stephen Fry! I had my real friends.

'For example when my mother died, they were the people who brought soup and carried the coats of the mourners and I thought we were proper sisters and brothers under the skin. But lots of people going through divorce find the same thing. It doesn't matter if you're the baddie or the goodie, the friends network which you think you've had your whole lifetime, for some reason, dissolves and disintegrates.

'A lot of them went with him and they had been my friends originally, I had grown up with them. They never picked a phone to explain what happened or say why. I still feel extremely upset about it and it was fifteen years ago.

'Yet people who I knew as periphery friends – people at work or that I didn't know terribly well – came through extraordinarily well, stepped up and seemed to empathise and understand. They were behaving as you would want people to behave while the people who I thought I could almost take for granted, so endemic was our genuine love for one another, just disappeared in a puff of smoke.'

Vanessa Feltz, 2014

———◆———

'I believe women should support each other. I have gained so much in my life through my mother, my daughters and friendship with other women and I think it's in our strength, the way we nurture, support and communicate with each other.'

Angelina Jolie, 2016

'I loved my work in the theatre from the very beginning, and I've always been on the happiest terms with those with whom I have worked. There is no comradeship more delightful than that which comes from association with people all working for the success of a play.'

Dame Lillian Braithwaite

———◆———

'My life is about me becoming a woman now and all the wonderful things that I'm getting to do in my womanhood, which is spend time with my friends, travel the world, learn about culture, become political, philanthropic and work really hard.

'I love my past. I embrace it with so much love because I wouldn't be the person I am today without it. But I am completely looking forward.'

Drew Barrymore, 2007

Baroness Shirley Williams and her friend Helge Rubinstein
shared a house even after they were married and had children
of their own. As aspiring politician Shirley had one child and
Helge had three, Helge did most of the childcare. In 2014
the two women talked about their enduring friendship, which
began at Oxford University in the 1960s.

Shirley: 'Helge was the rock on which it was all built and she
was the one that had the great feeling for raising children.
But the great thing was the children all melded together
and what it meant was I had an absolute feeling of security
so if I was summoned to the House of Commons to vote
at midnight, which happened quite a lot at that time, I could
just ring and say "I can't get back" and I knew that Becca
would be fine, there would be people to look after her
and so on. I think we were much less helpful to Helge and
[husband] Hilary than they were to us and Helge put more
into it than anybody else but she never counted the cost
and we didn't either. It was a very happy set-up.'

Helge: 'Shirley was a great support to me when Hilary
died because I knew she loved him too and that was very
important. Hilary and Shirley had been friends for a very
long time so it was a loss to her too so it felt good that
someone felt similarly. When Hilary died, which he did
quite suddenly, the one person I felt I could ring up at one
in the morning was Shirley. I knew she'd be there for me,
at any time.'

Shirley Williams and Helge Rubinstein

Agony Aunt Deidre Sanders has been answering letters about relationship problems in her Dear Deidre column since 1980. In 2014, she appeared on Woman's Hour *and addressed the question of Facebook 'friends'.*

'I think we ought to have a separate word. It's almost clever marketing on Facebook to call them "friends". "Acquaintances" doesn't really work so there ought to be another word for what a lot of people get on Facebook. From a subjective side of it I think it's really important that people distinguish between real friends – from whom we need warmth, affirmation of our values, the sort of people we can turn to in times of trouble, who we know will always be understanding and caring and loving, even if we've messed up – and that's very different to what some people get on Facebook. People can be very isolated and are trying to convince themselves on Facebook or other social media sites that they're getting real friendship out of this and actually they are masking a problem which is that they haven't got any real friends. If they step outside their door there isn't anyone they can turn to who will love them.'

Deidre Sanders

'I'm a big fan of friendship pruning so if I have friends in my life and I come to realise I don't get out of them what I want, and maybe vice versa, I tend to freeze them out. I don't do it brutally, I don't have a massive argument about it unless there was something in their behaviour that caused me to do that. But I would stop replying to texts, be very evasive about when to meet up again and be nice, but basically push them out gently.

'There's no point in having friendships in your life that don't make you feel good about yourself.'

Novelist Jo Carnegie, 2015

'I think female friendship and the way people value it has changed enormously over the years. When I read about the 50s and the 60s, female friendship was considered to be a woman popping round to her neighbour's house for a cup of tea and cake while the kids were at school and talking about their husbands' careers and recipes.

'Now what has happened is that people have started to realise, and men have started to realise, that female friendship is incredibly powerful and must be valued.'

Dawn O'Porter

'The Sisters of Perpetual Disorder are five women and me. We have a circle of women. By the way, every woman in the world should have a circle of friends. And if those circles were connected, if we have a million circles connected, we would change the world.

'These five women and I meet on Tuesdays. We pray. We come from different denominations. We are not religious people. But we think that positive thinking can help people who are sick or in distress.

'We witness each other's lives. We are always in touch through email or the phone. And we help each other. It's not group therapy. It's just a sisterhood in the old-fashioned way. And it has changed my life. I was always a foreigner when I moved away from Chile. I was a foreigner in Venezuela for thirteen years. And I was a foreigner in the United States until I met this group of women. And now I have roots there. I have my sisters.'

Chilean auther Isabel Allende, who fled Chile during the military coup of 1973 and eventually settled in the US

'I am relentlessly, burningly, nearly murderously ambitious. If it came to a choice between getting where I wanted to be and treading on my best friend, I wouldn't give my best friend a fifty-fifty chance.

'One fellow fashion editor is genuinely a close chum. If she were ill, broke, unhappy, I'd run my blood to water to help her out. I mean that. But when we're on a job together I'd all but break her leg before she got a better story than me. I'd fib to her, put her on the wrong scent, give her the wrong contact. She would – and has – done the same to me.'

Journalist Jean Rook, 1966

'An awful lot depends on having good friends and good family and sometimes that comes down to putting the effort in to bringing up a family and keeping in touch with brothers and sisters and it can also come from putting in some effort in your local community, being a volunteer and making friends like that. You have to put the effort in yourself, you can't just sit there and let it come to you.'

Edwina Currie, 2016

In 1940, when Vera Brittain wrote Testament of Friendship *about her close bond with the author Winifred Holtby, she said she felt that female friendship had been 'mocked, belittled and falsely interpreted'. In 2014, her daughter, Baroness Shirley Williams, reflected on female friendship at that time.*

'[My mother] was reacting to the general picture of the time, very much reflected in the films of the thirties, that women always fought each other for men. Maybe that was affected a bit by the losses of the First World War – there weren't as many men around – but the picture of women scrabbling out each other's eyes in order to get the lad they both wanted was very common. There was a widespread belief that women couldn't be friends, that their nature was to fall out with each other. And it was such a lie.

'She was there through Winifred's pretty awful death. They were very different characters but they were hugely supportive of each other and through the whole period from when they first met until Winifred died at the very early age of 37, there was a colossally intimate relationship. It was a very deep friendship of the type that has always been accepted for men but never for women.'

Baroness Shirley Williams

'My best friend lives in Australia and when I see her we just "are". It's lovely. It's the one relationship where if we don't see each other for three years there's no explaining to do. We just fit into this way of being which is very neutral, very easy and very lovely. I think for a woman it's very important to have that solidarity with somebody.'

Dawn O'Porter

'Unlike what we might call social media friendships, we would define friendship as a whole lot deeper than that. You got back to your shared values, your shared friendships, your shared loves and those become the background for a very rich relationship.'

Baroness Shirley Williams

'With partners we've got a whole different level of investment in the relationship, we've got a sex life going on and there's more complexity to it. But with a friend what we are often looking for is positive affirmation of how we see ourselves and feedback about the good side of ourselves. Often they are reaffirming our values more than our partner is. Opposites attract so your partner may be very different from you but you won't probably have friends with different values from you because you won't feel comfortable.'

Deidre Sanders, 2015

———◆———

'There's a huge guilt thing with women and maybe we feel part of the sisterhood. In a relationship, or working relationship, if we're not happy with something we will confront people and have it out but with women and friendships, we feel like we're the bad person even if they're not being a very good friend to us. We have this romantic illusion about friendships and we cling on to things that are past their sell-by date.'

Novelist Jo Carnegie

'I now cast my net further afield and I don't think that friends have to have a certain blueprint to be friends. I think before, I imagined you had to have a shared background and a shared geography but now I don't think so. Any human who wants to be a friend and proffers the hand of friendship is extremely welcome to be a friend of mine.'

Vanessa Feltz

HOME TRUTHS

Home is where the heart is but, in the 70 years Woman's Hour *has been on the air, the shape of the average household has seen considerable changes. In 1946, when the first show was broadcast, most married women stayed at home and raised children and the husband, very much the head of the household, was almost always the breadwinner. In the 21st century home, both partners are likely to be working, a wife may well earn more than her husband and most modern men even do their fair share of the chores.*

Here are some of the voices, past and present, who provide a snapshot of domestic life.

'I think a room should reflect the owner's way of living and look practical and *used*. Heaven knows, mine does.'

Comedienne Joyce Grenfell, 1946

'You may marry, as I have done, and continue your nursing career and when you have children you will find that motherhood will be less of a problem because of what you learnt when you were training. I found that although I had never done any housekeeping or cooking, and hadn't a clue about the details of making a home, my nursing training stood me in good stead when I first embarked on the business of being a housewife.'

Agony Aunt Claire Rayner, 1958

'There are days when I want to be a housewife doing purely domestic jobs. I can't tell you how much I long sometimes just to have a morning at home to practise my cooking. At the moment I am simply dying to make a cake.'

Celebrated actress Dame Edith Evans pines for the kitchen in 1949

'People have presumed that I'm writing about the joys of housework and how domestic life is the only true and proper way for a woman to achieve anything worthwhile ... It's seen that you must be perfect at everything, you must be wonderful. And actually what I'm saying is women are interested in the world at large, we operate in the world at large, but we also have domestic sides and we enjoy that too. And the idea is not that you do everything brilliantly but you are allowed to do a bit of everything.

'If I bake a cupcake, how many points does it knock off my IQ? What I'm never saying is, let's put on our fluffy mules and a pair of baby dolls and pretend to be stupid and just bake.'

Nigella Lawson, on her book *How to be a Domestic Goddess*, published in 2000

'My husband was very funny about a dishwasher. We had
the first one when the house was built and back then,
in the 1960s, Bob didn't believe in them and he very
virtuously said, "I will do the washing up" and I thought,
"Ha, ha, ha!" Anyhow, he made us all eat a cooked
breakfast, with mustard on the side, and armed with
these dirty plates we went down to the dealer's to have a
demonstration – would they get the mustard off? Well, of
course, it did it beautifully, I knew it would.'

Marguerite Patten, 2009

'I liked the traditional duties of keeping a house. I'm not
the greatest at it in the world but I loved doing it. It was
inviting people to come to your home and therefore it
mattered to me what china we used, what the flowers
looked like and what the menu was.'

**Former First Lady Hillary Clinton and
presidential candidate talks about
entertaining at the White House, 2003**

'More and more we see younger men doing the cooking, looking after the kids, changing their nappies, accepting all the responsibilities, the unattractive responsibilities, of raising children as well as the lovely ones. And I know among the contemporaries of my son-in-law, for example, and my nephew-in-law, you do get now a much greater recognition that men are part of the family. I think that's wonderful. I also think it's the only way to save the desperate incoherence of young men who don't know what they're for.'

Baroness Shirley Williams, 2004

Screen icon Bette Davis may have played some of the most heartless women in the history of cinema but, away from the studio, the mother-of-three insisted she was all heart. The Baby Jane *star, who died in 1989, spoke to* Woman's Hour *ten years earlier, when she was 71.*

'I love animals and I'm a soft and loving mother. People get me tangled up with the parts I have played because we are all attracted to evil.

'But I'm very domestic. I love my home and everything about a home. I have had the luck of having three children and I now have grandchildren. I don't need to work all the time. I'm glad I have it now that the children have married and are grown up because I think one should keep going for one's brain. I think I'm very fortunate once the family is gone that I have a profession. Any woman who has is very fortunate or else you have nothing left. I would have nothing without my family. My children are definitely what makes me happy today.'

Bette Davis, 1979

'So you see what purposeful daydreaming can accomplish.
My advice is, try it. Dream of what you want most and
dream of it really hard, when you're tackling the washing,
when you are cleaning out the ashes, when your hands are
full of cinders and your teeth are on edge, or when your
back is breaking in the garden.

'Daydreaming – that's just a hazy indefinite imagining,
no good at all. You've got to work at it. But I must warn
you, it may not be exactly as you dreamt. It may be like
my dream of the wonderful, big house, standing in its own
grounds. I got it. But I forgot to dream up the servants
and the gardener.'

**Catherine Cookson after publishing her
first novel, 1950**

'I truly consider that home is where I'm working,
wherever my children are, wherever Katy goes to school:
that is home.'

Joan Collins, 1984

'I think the best advice is to outsource as many domestic chores as you can afford. It's not always possible for everyone, and it's not possible for me, but it's very good advice. And avoid the rows.'

Lucy Mangan, author of *The Reluctant Bride*, reflects on advice from Jilly Cooper's marriage manual, *How to Stay Married*, 40 years after it was first published in 1969

———•◆•———

'I think men have changed a great deal. I think the younger generation of men has really become much more involved with their children. I do not believe that men are full participants in the household, or full participants in childcare. I don't think they give 50 per cent, but the fact that they give anything is remarkable compared to the way they used to be.'

Author Marilyn French, 2006

'I'm not really cut out just to be a housewife and nothing else because of all my years of being in the business, through my teenage years. Obviously I would like to have a family and this is something I'd have to sort out when the time came. But in the meantime, I like to try and involve myself in as many things as I can.'

Singer Helen Shapiro

———◆———

'It's a working kitchen and people are often very disappointed when they see it. I remember one reporter coming and saying, "I had a picture of you in a rocking chair." I said, "In a rocking chair! How on earth would I cook in a rocking chair?" But we've never had a family kitchen out here. The two rooms where we gather are the dining room and the sitting room. This is where I work.'

Marguerite Patten shows *Woman's Hour* host Jane Garvey her hallowed kitchen in 2009

'One of the advantages of being divorced is that you're not exactly a mother and you're not exactly a father, you're suddenly a sort of leader of the troop. And quite often, or certainly in my case, there's a whole new family relationship with far more family discussion. As a result of it my sons have grown up to be far more responsible than I was at their age.'

Shirley Conran, who raised her two sons alone after her divorce from designer Sir Terence Conran in 1962

'I think [my husband] might be deprived of the sort of really agreeable, easy comforts that one might expect out of married life. I mean that, in effect, he can't expect to come home to a dinner which is waiting for him when he gets back. It's probably a dinner which I rush in, cook and rush out again. He's obviously going to miss some of the possibility of somebody listening sensitively to what's happened during the day. I'm not sure how much that really happens anyway, but let's present a sort of ideal marriage for the moment. Instead of which we find that one of the things you've got least time to do is to talk to each other as much as we would like. When we're together, we talk our heads off because we never run out of conversation, but there's never quite enough time.'

Baroness Shirley Williams, in 2004, on her marriage to Bernard Williams

'I am very old and we were different back then so before Leo got home at 5.30 I would tidy up a bit, make sure my underwear wasn't on the floor and put the potatoes on. But I think [the chores] should be halved. You've got to be brave as a woman. You've got to ask and say "please, please, please pick up your socks." We're very wet.

'It's the same with sex. Women are very bad at asking for what they want. They think men should know and should bumble along finding out. If I was coming back in another life I would ask people to do things. Very nicely, but one tends not to do it.'

Author Jilly Cooper, 2016

Prue Leith wed second husband John Playfair in October 2016, but the couple continue to live in separate houses.

'He lives a mile away from me. He has a house and I have a house and he is a fantastic collector of books and what I would call junk and he would call wonderful memorabilia, so he's got a lot of stuff. I'm rather neat and tidy so I don't want that stuff in my house and he doesn't want me tidying his house. So he stays with me and in the morning, he gets up, he feeds the dogs and he goes home and does all his ironing, cleans his shoes and he keeps all his gear there. It's the ideal thing. What I get is him but without his clobber and without the responsibility of having to look after his laundry or sew on his buttons.'

Prue Leith, 2016

'English women don't assert themselves. No matter what their status and social position every woman in England has become a housewife … yet they don't begin to know what they deserve. If British women want something they should be firm and stand together and there won't be a housewife in the world that won't uphold them, because of the way they carried on in the war and ever since. I don't think they realise their own splendid courage and they deserve every consideration and the highest praise.'

Actress Gertrude Lawrence, 1949

'There came a time when I naturally wanted to marry and have children. "You cannot marry and have a career" they said. These ogres. I thought, naively, men marry, work and have children. Truly they said, "But you are not a man, you must choose." What ghastly tyranny this choice between the work that one loves and the natural, normal life for a woman, which usually means a man, children and home.

Well I did marry, I've had my children, two boys and two girls, and I continued working at music, by day and by night if necessary … It has been thought unnatural – a woman's place is in the home etc. For me this combination of composing and running a home has become quite normal, and I hope it will for my daughters, too.'

Pioneering female composer
Elisabeth Lutyens, 1949

'When a woman is married and has young children it seems to me that her first responsibility is to her home and those children. A family unit is very, very important to the guidance and direction that children need, especially during those formative years. But we must remember also that there are a numbers of women who will never get married, so should they just stay at home and take care of the pots and pans?'

Shirley Chisholm, the first black woman elected to the US Congress, 1971

'Fortunately, we have a small house and so it doesn't need a great deal of attention. Of course things get untidy and a house always does when it's lived in. That's just inevitable and things aren't kept as perfect as otherwise one would wish. But then we are all doing what we want to do and when we all get home at night we talk about it.'

Conservative leader and future PM Margaret Thatcher, 1976

'I wander through life with my head in a cloud. I found out when I got married you simply couldn't do that, that if you weren't neat and orderly – I think order is almost more important than being neat – and if you didn't have some pre-planning then you were just laying up trouble for yourself later on.

'It's very difficult with young children when life is chaotic. You have to decide whether you have ornaments or children.'

Shirley Conran

———◆·◆·◆———

'A housewife has to be a secretary, an ambassador, all sorts of things. A house is almost like a country and you have to play twenty different roles to run the house.'

Yoko Ono, 1973

THE WORKPLACE

By its very nature, Woman's Hour *plays hosts to guests from all walks of life and covers a huge range of careers and professions. Here some of the many guests share the stories and experiences gathered in their own fields of expertise.*

'Sometimes I'm thinking, "Who can I seat next to Donatella [Versace] at dinner?" And at the same time I'm trying to lug the bin bags out and the cat's just been sick and I think, "This is not how people think it's going to be."

Former *Vogue* editor Alexandra Shulman on the glamorous life of a magazine editor

---

Edith Summerskill became a Labour MP in 1938 and went on to become a government minister in 1945. In 1967, she was interviewed by Joan Yorke who asked her how hard it was to bring up two small children while serving as an MP.

'It's very, very difficult. The male Member of Parliament has his wife in the constituency, organising bazaars, doing his secretarial work, smiling sweetly at difficult constituents but a woman, of course, if she's married and has a home, like all women who work outside the home, does two jobs. But don't forget we do it willingly.'

Edith Summerskill

'Real life does have to come first because writing isn't life. If they [the children] don't come first, I really don't think you would have much to say. It does seem to me that is one of the advantages women have over men when they're writing. Men have wives who look after everything and I think this is a great pity.'

Novelist Fay Weldon on writing while raising her three sons 1974

———◆———

Betty Boothroyd served as the first and only female Speaker of the House of Commons, from 1992 to 2000. In her youth, she had been a member of the famous dance troupe The Tiller Girls which she claimed was a help when she first landed the Deputy Speaker position in 1987.

'I'm tall, I wear high heels and I think that helps me to assert myself. But I think more than it helping in terms of being assertive, I think assertiveness comes with personality. I think the fact of the discipline, which I've always enjoyed, and the teamwork, I think that is coming into play very much now.'

Betty Boothroyd

'We spoke to the entire world without words. We had to be articulate somehow with our bodies and faces. [D.W. Griffiths] kept telling us that a kitten, a puppy or a tear or a smile will be understood, but the subtler things, you must be very careful and study the animals for the subtler things, because our stories were quite elemental.

'We were so starved for new gestures and ways of being surprised or happy, I found myself haunting insane asylums and any place where I could get a new kind of a hand gesture, a facial expression, or body move.'

Lillian Gish on acting in silent movies

'The nice thing about being a writer is that you never really know who your readers are. Being a writer is like standing on a desert island and putting a message into a bottle and throwing the bottle into the sea, and hoping that somebody will find the bottle, open it up and be able to read the message. But you never know.

'When they find the bottle, some of them read the message upside down and backwards, but a lot of them seem to read it the right way up.'

Margaret Atwood

'I'm always frightened of this word, "creative", because I think almost everybody and almost every job is creative. I think we're very mad the way we sort of label only certain things as creative, and businessmen can be very creative but I think it's difficult to think of a job that isn't creative, and yet we seem to only apply it to certain things.

'Presumably as a lawyer one could be very inventive and creative. I think one could apply it to anyone.'

Fashion designer Mary Quant, 1971

'I yearn after a picture to go back on the stage. It does take a total physical involvement, and when I was at drama school, part of the training had a lot to do with modern dance and fencing and gymnastics and clown work, all this kind of stuff. You could really throw yourself into a part there. It's true, sometimes the biggest thing you'll do is pick up a teacup and put it down, that's the most physical you'll get, and a lot of it is because of the size of the picture. Your eyebrow is magnified 10,000 times.'

Oscar-winning actress Meryl Streep

Dame Stella Rimington was the first female head of MI5 and, on her appointment in 1993, became the first to be publicly named. In 1999, she revealed the unexpected fallout of the decision to go public.

'I think we didn't really guess quite how much interest there was going to be and the great level of press attention that actually drew attention to me, and particularly to where I lived, and did present a serious threat to our security, because at that time we just lived in an ordinary London street. Very rapidly we had to move and effectively go underground, which was a rather strange reverse when one had been trying to be more open.

'The neighbours looked at it in two ways. Some thought it was rather exciting to have a famous person living in the street. Others, however, thought that this famous person was actually bringing danger to them and their children, and made it pretty clear to me – some of them, anyway – that they would rather I wasn't living as their next-door neighbour.

'We had to sell that house and go somewhere where we actually lived anonymously. It was a rather strange reversal, because we'd always just lived like anybody else in an ordinary London street, and my neighbours just thought I was that nice, quiet lady who went off to work every day like everyone else.'

Dame Stella Rimington

'When I was making films there was a time when the only parts that were available for women that were good parts were either psychopaths or adulteresses or alcoholics or something like that. And I vowed that I would never be in a film that would embarrass my children.'

Shirley Temple Black, 1976

———◆◆◆———

'Maya Angelou says, "When you know better, you do better." So in my early years I was just grateful to be a woman, being allowed to do that job alone because for my first years in television nobody thought I could do it alone so I always had a co-host who was male. He would tap me when I was allowed to speak and that would give me permission and then I could ask a question. I hated it but I didn't question it because I just thought, "I'm not going to be here forever."'

Chat show queen Oprah Winfrey, 1999

'Writing a novel is like falling in love. It's a total commitment. It's hard. It's scary at the beginning. When I am into it, it's fine, but getting into it, it's very hard.'

Novelist Isabel Allende

———◆———

'There is a particular air of authority that a woman has to bring when she does the news. And this authority, especially in the earlier days, can be interpreted as aggressiveness; isn't she tough, isn't she hard, boy, look at those questions she asks. And I would like people to know that I can bleed too, that I am a person as well. I don't mind this in the public; I think the public really does know me if they watch enough and the public is very intelligent and very kind. I'm speaking more of our critics. They are so much out for the attack, especially these days and there I would wish that everyone would realise – and I try to myself in interviews – that we are talking about human beings.'

News anchor Barbara Walters

'[*Roseanne*] was something that I wasn't terribly keen on doing but I was sort of talked into it because I do like doing comedy and it's something that I want to do. And I met Roseanne [Barr] and I don't think I endeared myself to her because I said that the tattoo on her husband's chest looked like another actress called Brenda Vaccaro!'

Actress Joan Collins on her cameo in *Roseanne*

'I wanted to become an archaeologist but became gradually put off by it, partly because it was increasingly difficult for Jews to go and work in some of the countries in the near East and partly because when I went and took part in digs in England, I found it was mainly just scraping bits of stone and wasn't fantastically interesting!'

Rabbi Julia Neuberger

'The [careers advisors at school] still thought that girls, particularly girls from the ethnic background that I had, should have limited aspirations. And I was working in Sainsbury's as a Saturday girl, and they thought that if I really worked hard and applied myself with energy, one day I might rise to the dizzy heights of being a supervisor.'

Baroness Scotland, 2004, who became the first black woman to be appointed a Queen's Counsel before taking up several ministerial posts in the Labour government. She is now a member of the House of Lords

———◆———

As Ripley in the 1979 sci-fi epic Alien, *Sigourney Weaver became one of the few women to have played the lead in an action movie. In 2016, she looked back on the impact the film had.*

'We did [*Alien*] when women were moving into a lot of areas we hadn't been. A lot of physical jobs in the armed services, in industry and even in the board room and jobs in government that women hadn't been in before. I think that Ripley represents a normal person who is doing her job and is thrown into an impossible situation. She's an everyman character and it's rare that a woman gets to play an everyman character.'

Sigourney Weaver

'When the Second World War first started, when it was declared, I thought, "There goes my career, I shall finish up in a factory or the army or somewhere." You imagined all the theatres and everything closing down, which didn't happen, except when the sirens sounded and everybody, if they wanted, they could stay in the theatre and the show would go on and then afterwards, if the raid was still on, they'd come up on stage and we'd have a little dance and a sing-song.'

Dame Vera Lynn, the Forces' Sweetheart, speaking in 2002

'There were quite a lot of women working in MI5 but they were regarded as second class citizens, I have to say, in those days. There were two career structures, one for men and one for women and, as a woman, one could never really rise beyond being what was effectively a support worker. One was thought to be okay to deal with the papers – I could say, to type and make the tea, but it was a bit more than that. But women were not regarded as suitable to do the sharp-end intelligence work, to go out on the streets and try to recruit and run the human sources of information, for example. That was regarded as men's work.

'It changed gradually over the years and began to change very shortly after I joined. But now, and by when I left, women were working in all the areas of the service, even in the most dangerous. I remember being told at one stage by one of my bosses that dangerous work is not for women. However, all that's changed now and women do all the different jobs that the service offers. And, of course, they do them differently from men but I would say just as well, and they provide the diversity that an organisation needs.'

Dame Stella Rimington on MI5 in the 1960s

'I would like to register a complaint. I do wish smoking was forbidden in all the theatres, as it is in America. It would make all the difference in the world to us and to the audience. They wouldn't cough so much, they wouldn't fidget so much and they wouldn't distract the attention of those around them by striking matches and flicking lighters. Sometimes it's like acting in front of a forest of fireflies!'

Actress Gertrude Lawrence on British theatres in 1949

'To any girl who thinks she would like to be a nurse, but is worried about some aspects of it, I would say this. Try it. If you are really unsuitable the hospital will soon tell you, if you don't find out for yourself. If you *are* suitable you will find that you can have just as much fun and meet just as many eligible men as your sisters in a nine-to-five office job.

'Don't be ashamed of your wish to have fun and meet young men. It is quite normal at your age, and very important too, if in your turn you wish to become a wife and mother.'

Nurse and Agony Aunt Claire Rayner, 1958

'As soon as a baby girl is born in America she is wrapped in a pink blanket and the decision is made for her that she must become a secretary or typist or whatever it might be. The people in America seem to feel that this is the prescribed role for women just as for many years they felt the prescribed role for blacks was in the menial services. So many women can't accept women moving into the political arena, or women moving into other arenas, because many of these women have never known any other kind of world.'

Shirley Chisholm, 1971

'Ever since I could talk I wanted to perform. If there was a party I was one of those horrible kids who wanted to be in the front and do a dance and sing.'

Singer Cilla Black, 1965

'The job of the Speaker lies somewhere between being a bungee jumper and a trainspotter. Sometimes it's very dull and you think instead about what you are doing at the weekend or the weekend shopping list, and you take your eye off the ball for a moment. That's when all sorts of things break loose.

'Then of course there's the bungee jumping – you never know if you are going to jump into difficulties or not, so every word has to be guarded.'

**Speaker of the House of Commons,
Betty Boothroyd, 1994**

'There is an interesting female adjective used about us and that is "tough". I think that if we were men people would perhaps say we were strong because of what we have to do. If you're producing you have to make a lot of quick decisions or you drive people insane and you must appear to have no doubts. So you get the reputation of being decisive and if you're female the adjective they use is "tough".'

Presenter and producer Esther Rantzen, 1978

'Television is an absolute phenomenon because it goes into everybody's home all over the world. If I actually sat and thought, before I did any scenes in *Dynasty*, how many millions of people were going to see it, I think I would have been so terrified that I would never have got out of the make-up room.'

Joan Collins, 1984

'Some of the boys I met had been out for six years. They used to say to me, "If you're here, England isn't so far away."'

Dame Vera Lynn on meeting the troops in the Second World War

CHANGING
THE WORLD

When Woman's Hour first aired in 1946, married women were still barred from many jobs, only a third of women worked and the recently published Beveridge report had concluded that the married woman should not seek 'gainful employment outside of the home' because 'she has other duties'. But changes were afoot with women who had been given a taste of work during the war years reluctant to step aside for their returning men and campaigns for equal pay gaining ground. With men in charge of industry and just 24 female MPs out of a total of 640, however, the women's movements were still reliant on male supporters to make major changes. Today, 70 years on, sisters really are doing it for themselves.

'Power is not something I spend a lot of time thinking about. I just get on with the job. But I suppose the point is, in the role I'm in I am making decisions that will affect people's lives. That's what power is.'

Theresa May, 1993

'There really aren't enough women in politics and those of us that are in long for the day there are so many of us that we shan't be a phenomenon any more.'

Margaret Thatcher, 1993

'As a young child, I started to realise that girls didn't have
the power, or people wouldn't listen to us in the same way
they'd listen to boys. I couldn't articulate it then, but I felt
all these things bubbling up in me. I decided I was going
to spend the rest of my life dedicated to fighting for equal
rights and opportunities for boys and girls, men and women.'

Billie Jean King

'What I think many people would recognise was that
home, family, kids – *Kinder, Küche, Kirche* – would not
be enough for me. Would not be enough for a lot of
women. Back in the 1970s, when I was keen to do all this,
the majority of women with children under eleven were
still at home, or perhaps only working part-time. By the
time I got to the House of Commons in 1983, I was the
only woman member of the House with young children
and a seat outside London. I was a freak. Yet there were
millions of women like me all round the country, and it
was about time the House of Commons recognised that
they should be represented.

'The world of politics in those days – and still, to some
extent now – reeks of double standards, it reeks of
prejudice, and it's about time it stopped.'

MP Edwina Currie, 2002

'Nobody was more distressed than I was that I should have been the first woman in the House of Commons because I am a proud Virginian and I realised that, no matter how long an Englishwoman lived in Virginia, I wouldn't want her to be the first in the legislature.'

Nancy Astor, 1956

'I've always taken the simple view that, on a day-to-day basis, you get on with doing the job. Yes, you have aims and things you want to achieve, but just get on and do it and don't think too much about these other things. I'm not a calculating individual.

'I'm just interested in getting on with the job I'm doing at the moment.'

Theresa May, on being asked in 2013 if she would like to be Prime Minister

'We raised the glass ceiling and the equality isn't there but it's 100 times better than in my time, but the generations of women [who now work] a lot of them do feel quite victimised in the workplace and are quite fragile compared to what we were like. I think it's slightly gone pear-shaped because so many mothers work now, and can get the jobs, and yet there is a great distinction between how they are at home, worrying about their children, and how they are running a law firm. Somehow it's all on their shoulders.'

Anne Robinson, 2016

Author Doris Lessing joined the Communist party in London in the 1950s and spent many days knocking on doors to spread their message. But she wasn't overly impressed by their attitude to women's rights.

'I was canvassing at a great block of flats in Crowndale Road, and I was going from door to door. But what I found was that as they opened the door every woman said, "Oh, don't talk to me. Come and talk to my husband, who will be back at six." That was quite interesting. I'd come from the colonies. I wasn't used to this. But then they would tell me what ghastly lives they led. So this went on all day, if not more, than one day so I rang up the party, and I said, "I don't think that you realise that this town is full of women going mad behind closed doors." And, of course, they were totally uninterested. "What are you talking about? What rubbish is she talking about?" That was the reaction.'

Doris Lessing

'I think that my country, the US, still needs to have a good debate around abortion. There are robust [arguments] on both sides of that debate that still need to be had in our country, but I think what's happened is the church has attached abortion to contraceptives and made the entire discussion political and what I'm saying is no – abortion is its own thing and the contraceptive piece – that really is non-controversial.

'82 per cent of Catholics in the US think contraceptives are morally acceptable and the church is made up of its members, so when 82 percent think it's a non-controversial issue, for me that's good enough to say it's non-controversial.'

Melinda Gates, co-founder of the Gates Foundation explains to *Woman's Hour* why contraception is essential across the world and how this squares with her Catholic faith

'Often the song needn't have a message in its own words, but if you put it in a certain context, then it has a certain meaning. During those years when I sang "Joe Hill" and I was pregnant, and my then-husband was a Country and Western fan, so if I sang "The Green Grass of Home", which is the most totally apolitical song you could find and said, "This is dedicated to my husband who is in prison for refusing the draft for Vietnam," boom! Then all of a sudden that song, for that moment in the concert, becomes political.'

Singer and activist Joan Baez

———◆◆◆———

'Things have changed enough that young women's lives are much easier than they used to be. They can get into the schools they want to go to, they can get jobs, they can buy cars, they can buy houses. They can be independent, lead independent lives, and the only thing that's a little hard is getting a guy, and they want a guy, and the guys don't like feminism, so they're going to say they don't like feminism too. You know, that's not going to change except that not all girls are like that, and not all girls are willing to make that trade-off.'

Feminist author Marilyn French

'Women need more nurturing, more reassurance, they need more love. It's a tough sport, and at grassroots level, women would look after the needs of little girls better, because they understand them better. Maybe we would keep more girls in the sport longer, if we had more female coaches on every step of the pathway. But at the very top level, it is perhaps thought that the skills that women have don't transfer as well at the top end of sport where you have to be unbelievably tough.'

Judy Murray on coaching women

'I'd say I have a concern over lots of people, whether they should be parents or not, and actually disability for me doesn't figure high on the list. But I think it's just getting the message out there that disabled people do play a full and important part in society. They should be working, they should be in education, they should be contributing and they should be buying houses and part of that, that they should have a right to be a family.'

Paralympic athlete Baroness Tanni Grey-Thompson, 2012

'Punk was very much a culmination of research. Malcolm [McLaren] and I, we were looking at our own lifetime's culture for motives of rebellion, so we went to rockers, teddy boys, anything that was somehow or other not part of the establishment. When it was all put together, the look of an urban guerrilla, that's the look we wanted. So it's not iconoclastic, it was quite simply an exercise in youth against age.

'I changed at a point simply for the reason that I realised that we had been trying to somehow or other affect the establishment in some way, and what we had done is that we gave the establishment lots and lots of ideas to market, and so I realised that I did not want to be this token rebel.'

Fashion designer Vivienne Westwood

'A lot of designers and houses just seem to have forgotten about balancing and using models of colour so we're trying to make them aware. We're not attacking, we're not blaming, we're not pointing the finger, we're just saying, "Let's sit down and have a relationship and a conversation about this, because what's happened is it's coming across as a racist act. We're not calling you racist, but that's how it appears."

'When I started working in the late Eighties, I worked with so many beautiful, elegant black models and now it's just not like that. Now, you'll be lucky if you see one in a fashion show and it should not be that way.

'I hear horror stories – horror. There's one girl, I won't say her name, but she's very well known … She's told by a designer when she goes to do a casting, "We don't want United Colors of Benetton in this show". It's insulting and it's rude.'

**Naomi Campbell on the lack of models
of colour in fashion**

'When [the Labour party] said they were going to have a minister for women, I said, "Oh really. Are they going to have a minister for men?" Life is lived in families; it's lived in communities; it's lived in the place where you work. It's not separate men and women and I get really rather fed up with this.

'You don't live that way and I think it's quite wrong to give that impression. If you're sure of your talents and abilities you don't expect to be treated differently at work because you are a woman. The most able women I know, women who climb to the top whether it be in broadcasting, whether it be in business, whether it is as a woman editor, have got there by merit and that is their strength and their ability. Don't try and give the impression we need special treatment.'

Margaret Thatcher

'Pakistan is a Muslim country and I'm a Muslim. I'm proud of my heritage as a Muslim. I'm proud of my religion, but where I differ with the regime is in the exploitation of religion for political purposes, and I think that because repressive regimes need some kind of legitimacy, they sometimes exploit religion and put it forward as intolerant when it isn't. Then they put it forward as cruel when it isn't. I think really the matter of religion is between God and the individual, and whether one is a good Muslim or not a good Muslim doesn't depend on the state laws, it depends on the intention one has in one's heart to surrender before God's will.'

Benazir Bhutto

Baroness Scotland became a barrister in 1977 and was the first black woman to be made a QC in 1991. In 2004, she was asked how hard it had been to enter the legal profession as a black woman in the 1970s.

'It was no more difficult, perhaps, than if I'd chosen any other profession. Because I think what one has to realise is it was difficult for women and it was difficult for black women to enter almost any profession. If you look at journalism, any profession you like, and then you ask a very similar question, how many of us are there? And regrettably, the number is still quite few.

'It's not because black women lack talent and lack ambition. Sometimes, it's the opportunities that aren't easily obtainable.'

Baroness Scotland

'I think a few of us have [learned to take pleasure in our lives]. I think it's very rare, and I don't think it's just women. I think men don't either. I think my father did not know what real pleasure was. He knew duty. He knew what he had to do. I think that it's a concept that people haven't been allowing themselves because they were so full of ideas of what was righteous and good and the decent thing to do, and they tried so hard to be decent. I think a lot of men feel that pleasure is something female and the only way they can let themselves have pleasure is through power, which is why sex becomes such a power game for some men.'

Marilyn French

In 1947, former First Lady Eleanor Roosevelt recorded a special message for Woman's Hour *as part of her unceasing campaign to uphold human rights and give a helping hand to the less fortunate in society.*

'I think it is in the home that women really teach democracy; a home can be a miniature of what democratic life in the nation and between nations should be. And women who today are so closely tied in almost all countries to their home, to their children, have a very great responsibility … to take an interest in the civic and municipal general political situation as far as we are able to, not only because our opinions can carry weight, not only through the influence we have in our own circle, but through the way we can encourage the way other people manage their lives both at home and abroad. I always say at home that the woman's influence goes from her home out into the neighbourhood and her state and her nation and finally out into the world as a whole.'

Eleanor Roosevelt

Rabbi Julia Neuberger was Britain's second female rabbi and the first to run her own synagogue. In 1977, just five days after taking her post in Streatham, she explained how she had made such a huge step towards equality.

'Progressive Judaism argues that women and men are entirely equal and therefore in principle, there should be no objection whatsoever to a woman becoming a rabbi. However, it's taken quite a long time for this to come about.

'Orthodox Judaism does put women very much in second place within synagogue ritual, not necessarily in the home. And therefore it would've been quite impossible [in the orthodox religion].

Rabbi Julia Neuberger

'Why are we called babes? If you look at the women who are on the front bench and on our back benches, they're women of talent, they're women of energy and they're women of vision. And the women in our government have really delivered high-quality services. Not just for women but for all the people of our country. We've been inclusive.

'It's a very sad day when people want to describe you thus – a Blair Babe – instead of looking at what you actually do.'

Cabinet Minister Baroness Scotland, on being labelled as one of 'Blair's Babes' by the press

'I was born in a political household. I have breathed politics all my life and I have had the benefit of some very good education, both in my country and abroad, but the best education I would say I got in the prisons of Pakistan and being in Pakistan itself. I have gained tremendous experience. I can tell you it's not been easy. I have faced opposition from the military regime, and I have faced opposition from all those who were opposed to my father. There have been so many opponents, but I thank God and I thank the people for their blessings, and I thank my father for giving me the training that I have been able to outplay, outwit and out-manipulate all those who thought that they could use the Bhutto name as a figurative rubber stamp and take the support behind it.'

Benazir Bhutto

'The men are better than we are. The top men are better than the top women, but we never said we were better. Everybody keeps trying to stir it up, but we always said we're just as entertaining, and sometimes we're more entertaining and sometimes we're not as entertaining. But we never sold or branded ourselves on the fact that we're better than men. The men are much better than we are. That's a fact, that's a scientific fact, but we still, every person, human being has a right to be the best he or she can be.'

Billie Jean King on inequality in tennis

'Above all, don't think of yourself as "only a woman". Say instead: "I am a woman and proud of it." In my household it is I who keeps the peace so I am going to try and do the same thing, however humbly, in the world outside my house.

'You and I and people like us, who have learned to patch up family quarrels, are needed to do that very thing in politics and local government and parish councils and village institutes. In other words, we are needed as women.

'Once we get that idea into our heads and learn to believe in ourselves, we shall stop using men as yardsticks and stand on our own feet.'

Author Vera Brittain gives a rallying cry in 1953

———◆———

'There is no psychological test yet that indicates that either one of the sexes has a superiority of brain power. What we need is a combination and utilisation of the best talents and brain power of the two sexes. But we get ourselves lost and completely hung up on whether a person wears pants [trousers] or a skirt. It's ridiculous.'

Shirley Chisholm, who became the first black woman elected to the US Congress in 1968, speaking in 1971

'A lot of journalists have asked me if I'm a feminist but I ask them, "What do you mean by feminist?" and they go "er ... " because I think it's just a nice word to wave and to have as a flag.'

Joanna Lumley, 2013

———◆———

'Even my best friends couldn't talk to me, not in the House. I met Winston Churchill at dinner about two years afterwards ... and I said: "Why on earth didn't you speak to me?" He said: "We hoped to freeze you out." And then he added, "When you entered the House of Commons I felt as if a woman had entered my bathroom and I had nothing to protect myself but my sponge."

'I asked him: "Had it ever occurred to you that your appalling appearance might be protection enough?"'

Nancy Astor on becoming the first woman in the House of Commons in 1919

AGEING

Time waits for no man – or woman – and the effects of ageing come to us all. But Woman's Hour *is a safe space to share both the comical and alarming issues thrown up by advancing years as well as the wit and wisdom that comes with considerable experience.*

'When everything begins to look a bit random, hit the gym running. That's my advice.'

Felicity Kendal

————◆◆◆————

'I don't like the word retirement. I just don't think that's a nice word, and I think retiring is something I shall never do. It's very much like being in school. If you go from one grade to another, you don't call it the end, you call it the beginning. So actually, I wouldn't retire. I think that's like saying you're dying or you're about to die and sit in the corner.'

Ginger Rogers, 1969

'I appear to be able to put on half a stone in two days. It's incredible. But I'm not insecure about it. I write about it and I'm frustrated about it, and of course one would always like to be the half-stone smaller than you ever are, but I don't feel insecure about it and frankly I'm 58, I don't compare myself to those beautiful models at twenty. They're just different. I was never like that even at twenty.'

Former *Vogue* Editor Alexandra Shulman, 2016

———◆◆◆———

'I think that now I'm growing to be the cute old lady. It's like, "Ain't she a cute old lady? Ain't she feisty? Look at Debbie." I don't mind being cute because I think that when … it's hard to grow up with being Debbie and cute. It was hard for me to mature. But I am a mature woman and I think the people that know me accept me as that. People that don't know me expect me to still be cute little Tammy [from a 1957 film role], but we've come a long way.'

Debbie Reynolds, at 57, on her 'cute' image

'I feel like I had a very good run, you know? I only started taking care of my skin in my 40s really … I just took it for granted. I made some terrible fashion mistakes though, I know that.'

Marianne Faithfull, 2013

———◆◆◆———

'Nobody tells you that when you get older you get shorter. I don't match up to the height of my passport at all. I seem to shrink all the time.'

Marguerite Patten, 2009, explains why she can no longer reach the higher shelves in her kitchen at the age of 93

———◆◆◆———

'It was quite an achievement, *The Golden Notebook,* because I now look back and I think, "My God, how did I do that?" I couldn't do it now, you see. I haven't got any energy. None. None. So if I write a cunning page or two, I'm quite pleased with myself.'

Doris Lessing, aged 89, speaking in 2008

'It's absolutely marvellous. It was my idea, my choice and she was thrilled. And so, I get to watch her age and watch her grow older, and she's extraordinary. I mean, she gets cranky and throws her walker down the driveway and I think, "Well, goody! You know, maybe I'll have that much fight left in me when I'm 93."'

Joan Baez on living with her elderly mother

———◆◆◆———

'I would like to be remembered for having given some kind of pleasure to people. There is a wonderful feeling when you hear an audience laugh, or you see children enjoying *Mary Poppins*, to be very corny, or whatever. There's a marvellous feeling to say, "Gosh, I really helped them for one second forget that there was the washing to be done or whatever, and made them laugh." It's a good feeling.'

Julie Andrews, 1974

'I was so thrilled and touched to realise that I'm old and deserve this old lady thing, so I took it and I love it. Of course they can have it back if they want.'

Joanna Lumley answers criticism of her use of her free London travel pass for the over 60s, in 2013

'77 is hot. It's wonderful. But it's the knees and the hips, and I am surprised at all these sags in my face. I thought I was about 60 in my mind, really. I feel about 60, 62, 65 maybe.'

Acclaimed author Maya Angelou, 2005

'There are certain things I can't do and one of the things is to stand and cook for long periods of time. I used to get up at four in the morning and cook and it was a lovely peaceful time, a lovely thinking time.'

Marguerite Patten, aged 93 in 2009

'Reaching my sixties the thing was the bus pass, being able to travel all over Scotland on the bus. That was fantastic. I go everywhere. I don't drive, I've never driven so the bus pass has been as good for me as the Pill was in The Sixties!'

Liz Lochhead, 2016

———◆·◆·◆———

'I can't wait to see myself at 50. The goal for me is to become more of myself, to completely own myself. I think like most women I had what I call the "disease to please" for many years. My whole life was defined outside of myself on the terms of everybody else, what other people wanted me to do. I would accept awards I didn't want to receive, I would attend functions, banquets, seminars and I wouldn't have any moments to myself, not because I wanted to do it but because I thought that if I didn't they were going to think I'm a snob, or that I'm not nice or they're going to think, "Oh gee, this TV show has gone to her head", so I had to run myself crazy so that everybody would think I'm a nice person. But between 40 and 42 I finally got it and stopped.'

Oprah Winfrey at 45, in 1999

'I've got an invalid son and he takes up a lot of time. I have to feed him and his medicine, and my medicines and my doctors and my hospital visits. It's a way of life, being old. It's hard work being old.'

Doris Lessing

'I think that by age 70 I will probably have less energy and less things to write about. I find that my craft has improved by the fact that I've been writing for twenty-five years, but not my ideas or my creativity. And there is a point, I suppose, in everybody's career then you start going down the slope. So I hope to be able to see that point and retire.'

Author Isabel Allende

'All I hear is, "Oh she's sixty, what can she know? She must be out of it. She must have lost the plot." No one ever stopped to think how outrageous to say such things. You wouldn't say that about a sixty-year-old Norman Mailer or a sixty-year-old John Wayne.

'There is no role for a woman to play who has reached a certain age. She becomes socially redundant and the terrible thing is, under current predictions, I've got another forty years to live. Forty years of having "lost the plot" is not going to be much fun."

Germaine Greer, 1999

'Seeing Sophie as a mother is an extraordinary and lovely thing. Watching her becoming a parent has been exceptional because I think she just gets it right. She has such energy for her children and such love for them and I can see that – although there are four boys involved here – they are all allowed to be themselves, so it's wonderful to watch.'

Janet Ellis on becoming a grandmother to daughter Sophie Ellis-Bextor's children

'The best thing about getting older and reaching 70 is that you say "no". You don't feel obliged to do all the things you did earlier. In the political world, having retired from parliament, is that I can say when the heck I like now. There's no official line and I can use all the weight of experience. I understand what Tony Benn meant when he said he left the House of Commons in order to get involved in politics.'

Former MP Edwina Currie, 2016

'I like the independence I've been given at this age. I'm lucky that I'm still mobile and I thank God for that but it is true that my mother didn't have the same independence of movement. I can go out alone. I can go out with friends, I can go out with my partner and I don't have to ask permission. Seriously it really was the case in the fifties and even the sixties that a woman would need to explain why she wanted to go out on her own.'

Author and Booker Prize nominee Marina Warner

'I'm looking forward to being 70 and then I'll be saying, "Well I may be 70 but I feel like 69," and people will say, "We've heard that joke before."'

Poet Liz Lochhead, 2016

———◆◆◆———

'I've got more grey hairs and I can jump the queue.'

Architect Shaheen Choudhury-Westcombe

'I don't know if they're not getting enough but I often say to older women at signings, "If you don't like sex in a novel don't buy this one but if you do like sex in a novel there's a bit of bonking in the potting shed." Which book do they buy? They queue up for the one that's got bonking in the potting shed.

'I think there's a lot of evidence that older women don't only enjoy reading about sex, they like sex. There's a myth that after 45 women like to sit in the corner and knit. It's nonsense. They still go dancing, they still ride horses, they still do everything so why on earth wouldn't they still like love?'

Chef and author Prue Leith, 2016

'Don't underestimate the old. We're quite with it. In spirit I could be jigging around and doing *Strictly Come Dancing* and anything you like, it's just that my legs won't let me.'

Marguerite Patten, aged 93

ILLNESS AND
BEREAVEMENT

The loss of a loved one is the hardest challenge most of us face in our lifetime. The death of a parent, husband or a child is devastating and many guests have shared their own tales of grief and how they dealt with it over the years.

'"I Wish You Love" is my favourite song in the world. It will be played at my funeral and it's a message to my children. I hope they cry madly. I'll never know, thank God. Maybe they'll say, "thank God".'

Bette Davis, 1979

Mary Berry lost her nineteen-year-old son William, in 1989, in a car accident. In her 2016 takeover she gave sound advice to anyone struggling to know how to handle another person's grief.

'Letters, I think, for a bereavement. I've got used to it having lost William. We had so many letters and I learned then that really when I now write to people – because I'm at the age when a lot of my friends are popping their clogs – I always think, "Can I think of something that I remember about them, a funny occasion or how brilliant they were at that, or how they taught me that, or how proud you are?"

'The people who are receiving it want to hear happy memories that you've had of them and if you put that in a text or an email, it's gone. But I think the written word is such a personal thing and I think it's very well received.

'The advice I had many years ago from my boss at the time, because I thought I couldn't write recipes, she said, "Write as you talk," and so you write just as you're talking into that letter. If you send it in ten days, or if it's a bereavement, a month afterwards, how nice to get something in the post. I think it means a lot. Also, if you see the person in the street, cross the road and say something. Maybe somebody's lost their husband and it's just happened, and you see a great friend across the road and they think, "I won't go because I won't know what to say." You've only got to say, "I've been thinking of you at this time." It just helps.'

Mary Berry

'I think something that everyone who is married to or related to or living with someone who's ill always feels, which is the great burden of always having to be nice and not being the moaner, and I think that's inevitable.'

Nigella Lawson, interviewed while her first husband John Diamond was battling cancer in 1998. He passed away in 2001

————◆•◆————

'It's not just children, there are plenty of adults who are dealing with loved ones who are very much diminished by their disease and who long for a release for their loved one from the pain or the strangeness of being ill.'

Sigourney Weaver on dealing with terminal illness in a loved one

Scottish National Poet Jackie Kay was born in 1961 to a white mother and Nigerian father and was adopted. As an adult she met her birth mother, Margaret, who died in 2016.

'I went to her funeral but [the family] didn't want to introduce me as her daughter because they were worried about that. I read a poem at the funeral and they introduced me as the National Poet of Scotland, which was a bit strange. I wasn't in the funeral cars, I had to get my own car to go there, so there was a kind of semi-inclusion and semi not. I think that's hard on people and it's really to do with the idea of secrets and lies and then you stand up and you feel that you've colluded to some extent with that secret.

'But the main thing was that I felt my birth mother did a very brave thing in bringing me into the world and I was there just before she died and I felt that I helped her leave the world.'

Scottish poet Jackie Kay

'I think that most relationships, I'm afraid, are built around that thing where the woman takes charge of the looking after, to some extent, and I think maybe John would have been more scared of illness as an observer than I am in that way.

'I was speaking to someone about this, and he said that he thought all marriages or long-term relationships, there was a central question which is, "Whose turn is it to be baby?" and that the difficulty when someone's ill is that it's only that person's turn to be baby.'

**Nigella Lawson on her relationship
with John Diamond**

'I needed to have a manager so of course my husband, being a musician, used to see that the music was right and he would make sure that the sound was right in the hall and he would do all the arranging and seeing to the contracts and travel arrangements and everything so that I never had to pick up a phone. So when I lost him, I had to use the phone for the first time in many years. I had to get used to talking to people myself because he would always speak on my behalf so that was a difficult thing for me to get used to. But I've gradually got used to it now!'

Dame Vera Lynn

Dame Katherine Ollerenshaw was deaf from the age of eight but became a brilliant mathematician, the Lord Mayor of Manchester (1975–76) and a close advisor of Margaret Thatcher. Although she lived to be 101 her children Charles and Florence died before her, aged 58 and 26 respectively, and her husband Robert died in 1986. In 2004 she spoke to Jenni Murray about how maths helped her cope.

'It's no good grieving. You can grieve and you just get worse and worse and go on grieving. For me it was an act of will. I go to my desk and always at night I do some mathematics. I take some problem with me to bed at night and the answer is often there in the morning. Never go to bed at night worrying or grieving.'

Dame Kathleen Ollerenshaw

———◆◆◆———

'Whatever feelings you have when somebody dies are not good or bad, they just are. You can't have the correct feeling or the incorrect feeling. Our feelings are a little bit like the dashboard on a car, they are there to inform you where you're at, so you know to take great care of yourself or something else.'

Agony Aunt Philippa Perry

Actress Kate Beckinsale was just five in 1979 when her dad,
Porridge *star Richard Beckinsale, died suddenly of a heart*
attack. In 2016, she talked how his memory was kept alive by
his work.

'I was only five but I do remember, pretty well – because
when something cataclysmic happens there's a sort of
BC and AD situation – so I remember passably more
than I would have done if nothing had happened. But his
shows were repeated constantly for years and years so
he remained incredibly familiar and present in this slightly
fictitious way, and he never aged.

'Often he would pop up. I remember after the birth
of my daughter someone turned on the television and
there was a repeat of *Porridge* so it feels like he has always
popped up, oddly, at significant moments, which is nice.'

Kate Beckinsale

———◆———

'We were married 58 years and he's been gone now four
years. It's not quite the same. It never can be, without
your loved one with you.'

**Dame Vera Lynn, remembering
husband Harry in 2002**

FOOD FOR
THOUGHT

Whether you spend hours in the kitchen whipping up a Michelin-star-worthy meal or you live on takeaways and ready-meals, food is an area that affects all our lives. For some it is a passion and for others, a battleground. But one thing is certain – we all have to eat.

'When people complain a lot about food in England, I wish I could take them back to my childhood and see what it was like then, and how dull food in the winter was, with the limited amount of vegetables and what little fruit we had.'

Food writer Jane Grigson, 1982

———◆◆◆———

'I love cake, but I'm very careful when I eat it. I know it's so comforting to have a piece of cake. If a child has a piece of cake when they walk in from school, a small piece of cake, a small flapjack in their lunchbox, it's having just one and not all the chocolate bars and sweet drinks as well.

'I have cake, usually a piece of cake in the afternoon, but I don't have two, I don't open the tin and straighten it up like I used to. A balanced diet is what it's all about and you can certainly have cake, but in proportion to everything else.'

***Great British Bake Off* star Mary Berry, 2016**

'I thought if I wrote a cookbook, I would hate it. If I wrote about food, though, I would love it because people all over the world use food. Not just as fuel for our bodies, which we have to have, but we use it for the most subtle reasons, the most obvious reasons. We use it to flirt, we use it to make good impressions, we use it to apologise, we use it to bring warring sides together, we use it to impress other people. We use it sometimes just to tell ourselves, "I'm alright, Jack."'

Maya Angelou

'What Tom [Hanks] says is that these coffee places give people with absolutely no decision-making ability whatsoever, the ability to make six decisions just to buy one cup of coffee. Short, tall, light, dark, caf, decaf, et cetera, et cetera, so that people with no decision-making ability whatsoever can delude themselves into thinking that they're captains of industry just by paying $2.95 for some coffee.

'I happen to believe that, and that scene when it's screened in America gets a hand because people just agree with it. It's true.'

Director Nora Ephron on a scene from her movie *You've Got Mail*

'I think an interest in food only really began in the war when my mother lost the cook and the housemaid and the nanny and she had to do all their work herself and she loved doing it. We had delicious meals; we used to go out and pick nettles and make nettle soup, and we'd pick blackberries. With her I began to explore exciting new things just as they began to come back.'

Food writer Jane Grigson, who was eleven when the war broke out and lived through years of rationing

'I suppose there's an element we associate with childhood and although I'm the last person on earth to start glorifying childhood – I don't think it's a wonderful time – perhaps the baking is the best bit of it.'

Nigella Lawson on the pleasures of baking a cake

'The thing I hated as a child was Mother's salads, because they were so unlike everybody else's. A salad in Britain in the old days was always the same, it didn't matter where you went – lettuce, hard-boiled egg, radish – very nice. But Mother wouldn't spend money on tomatoes if she had blackcurrants and things in the garden so we used to have all sorts of fruits in our salads and my friends used to say, "Doesn't your mother make funny salads!" Grown-ups would politely say, "Very interesting." But it turned out she was way ahead of her time.'

Marguerite Patten, 2009

'We're all a bit transfixed by food and it's understandable that we're all obsessed by food because it tastes so nice and it's so cheap. But I think food is too cheap. I think luxury food is too cheap. What do I call luxury food? As a vegetarian, it's meat and fish and I think it's sold too cheap. I think the basics should be cheap and luxuries should be expensive, which means that the animals can be brought up properly.'

Actress Joanna Lumley, 2013

'People generally have certain views about what we should and shouldn't be eating and women in particular have a very difficult relationship with certain foods and foods that they feel they should deny themselves.'

Nigella Lawson

———◆———

'We've all become neurotic. We all have eating disorders. We do have a "relationship with food" and all of us, by mid-life, have organised our lives in such a way that we have a protocol and that's the way we manage because food has become threatening. It's attractive and we feel we have to resist it and it's a constant battle. I despair of this and I don't know how this happened. I'd love to go back to the days when we ate when we were hungry and quit when we were full.'

Lionel Shriver, author of *We Need to Talk About Kevin*, in 2013

'When I'm testing recipes, I do put on about a stone because it's all just eat, eat, eat and I often think something is so good that I eat the whole thing. But when I am not testing I eat balanced meals, lots of proteins, and only have cakes occasionally for treats. My everyday diet is not what's on the show. I don't eat chocolate mousse every evening.'

Celebrity Chef Lorraine Pascale, who specialises in cakes and puddings

'I didn't talk for six years. I was what is called a volunteer mute. I had gone through a sexual misuse and abuse, and I just stopped talking. So when I went to school, I was known to write on the blackboard. Any time the teacher asked, I would write on the blackboard.

'And that one day I went with a new teacher. She had known about me, but when I went to write on the blackboard, she said, "Don't you dare. How dare you? I've heard about you."

'The students always teased me, calling me "Dummy, dummy, dummy", but this time they were on my side. They said, "Oh, teacher, she doesn't talk and she'll write on the blackboard." The teacher said, "You will speak, I know you can speak. You will not bring that stupidness in my classroom. You will speak and you will speak here." And finally she wound herself up enough to get angry, and she reached up and slapped me, and I turned around and ran out.

'I ran to my grandmother, and my grandmother said, "What on earth, sister?" and I pulled out a little tablet which I kept on my waist, and I wrote, "The teacher slapped me." And grandmother asked me, "Where?" and I wrote, "Face," and she said, "Go to the well and wash your face," and when I did, I came back, she had put on a new apron and she said, "Let's go," and we walked up the hill to the school. I had never seen her so purposeful. We walked up and we went into the school building and she said, "Show me your class, sister." So I took her to the classroom and she saw Miss Williams, the teacher, and Miss Williams asked, "Yes? May I help you?" and my grandmother, who was really a country momma said,

"Yes, ma'am. Are you Miss Williams?" And Miss Williams was a small woman. My grandmother was over six foot. And she said, "Yes, I am." My grandmother asked her, "Are you somebody's grandbaby?" And she said, "I am someone's granddaughter." And my grandmother said, "Well, this child here, this is my grandbaby," and she slapped her. Not full force, just slapped her.

'The whole room came to a stop because none of the children had ever seen my grandmother raise a finger to anybody. She didn't even raise her voice. And my grandmother said, "Now, sister, I have done the wrong thing here. Nobody has a right to hit anybody in the face, but I was teaching a lesson. Now, you find your chair, you sit down and get your lesson." And she turned around and walked out.

'The caramel cake takes forever for make, and especially in those days and in the country. We didn't have brown sugar, so she had to make brown sugar. She had to make everything from scratch, and it would take four hours to do it all and let things cool and that. So she only made it once in a while, but it was my favourite thing, and when I came home that day, my Uncle Willie said, "Now, sister, go in there in the kitchen. There is something in there, bring it out." And I looked in the kitchen and there was this luscious, just beautiful caramel cake, and so I brought it out and my Uncle Willie said, "Now, sister, nothing can make up for being slapped in the face, but your grandmother made this cake for you to show you how much we love you, how precious you are."'

Maya Angelou, 2005

'When it comes to the microwave, if you don't regard it as some sort of magic, or some terrible thing, it's another way of heating, another way to use to cook food and you just put it in relation to that, find the things it does extremely well – which are some fruits like apples and some vegetable, such as leeks as well as fish and steamed puddings, which it does in eight minutes. So it had a great many advantages and you just have to pick out what it does well.'

Marguerite Patten, 2009

———◆———

'The biscuit tin shouldn't be handy. My lot, if I made a crumble, always used to stretch for the sugar, and I now put the sugar the other end of the kitchen and they're far too lazy to get off their bottoms and walk to the other end of the kitchen, so they have the crumble just as it is.'

Mary Berry

———◆———

'We know about comfort eating, which is actually a bit of a misnomer because it simply makes one feel more miserable and desperate. But comfort cooking is a way of pottering around in the kitchen making yourself feel better, maybe a bit more grounded.'

Nigella Lawson

WOMEN OF THE WORLD

Travel broadens the mind and Woman's Hour *loves to hear the global perspective on all the issues discussed on the programme. Whether it's the tales of a seasoned traveller or the experiences of a visitor from abroad, it brings the world a little closer to home.*

In 1996, Joan Collins revealed she had been spooked when she found herself in a 'haunted palazzo' while staying in Venice.

'I'm never going to tempt the spirits by saying that I do or I do not believe in ghosts. I can only say that it was a shared experience between seven or eight of us and it was quite terrifying, one of those experiences that make all of the gooseflesh all over your body rise. So I do feel that something was definitely amiss in that palazzo and it has been rumoured many times. As one of the old ladies said there, I said there's a bad woman, she said "She's a *maladonna*" and shivered and looked around. There was a painting of a woman who'd been murdered by her husband 400 years previously because he thought she was having an affair with somebody else. In actual fact she wasn't so she's haunted it ever since.'

Joan Collins

'I did a trip to India with my husband, and, in a very remote village in the middle of nowhere, a very, very poor woman gave me a little package. And when I opened these rags, inside was a newborn baby. And it was a baby girl. The driver that was driving us around took the baby away, gave it back to the woman, and pushed me into the car, and then I found myself driving away without realising exactly what had happened. My husband said, "Why would she give her baby away?" And the driver said, "It's a girl. Who wants a girl?"'

Chilean writer Isabel Allende on why she set up her own foundation for the empowerment of girls and women

'Naturally I love all the labour-saving conveniences over there – they give a woman so much more leisure. But in spite of that life in America is much more tiring! I know that when people first come to New York they say it's like Switzerland, the air is so invigorating. But after a few months you see them looking pretty tired.'

Gertrude Lawrence, 1949

'I was born in Hawaii, I was brought up there, I went to public school there and it was challenging and I knew there was a bigger world out there, I think that's what distinguished me from most of my classmates. I really was curious about the world.'

Bette Midler

———◆◆◆———

'I would say to young women today, "Go and look at the lives of lots of different women. Don't just look at your little community in North London or wherever it is. Have a look at women around the world. Maybe travel a bit and see what you think." The way other women live in other cultures can often bring a lot of joy.'

Edwina Currie, 2016

In 2010, comedienne Victoria Wood visited Laos with a charity dedicated to clearing the country of bombs left over from the Vietnam War.

'I went to the Plain of Jars, which is like Stonehenge but made of jars. It might be a giant supermarket — nobody really knows what it is. But it's these huge stone jars, some of which are tipped over and their lids are scattered but it's one of those baffling things because nobody knows why they're there or how long they've been there.'

Victoria Wood

———◆◆◆———

'One is never bored with an Arab. He's got human qualities. He is an individualist. The fact is that Arabs are extremely good company and everyone who has travelled to Arabia has always found them so. They have a great many noble qualities.'

Travel writer Freya Stark, 1965

'In this country [the UK] it was, at least at one point, probably even chic to be pacifist but that's a state that's never been reached in the United States and so where do you go from there? ... I think America is more of a threat to the world right now than any country because the way Americans have been acting is like a bunch of kids and much more so than the communists at this point, although I don't care for communism.'

Singer and peace campaigner Joan Baez, 1965

———◆———

'I never lived in a mansion and I never owned a home out there. Mr [D.W.] Griffith told us early, he said, "This is a very good place for your body, a very bad place for your mind and soul."'

Silent film actress Lillian Gish on Hollywood

'The truth is if you want very cheap clothes they are going to come with such a price on their heads. People think "it's only a T-shirt" but trace it back and you realise some of the wages those women [in Bangladesh] are paid and all that stuff has to be grown and harvested, cut and dyed, fashioned and stitched and brought back and sold into the high street – and still only £2. Sorry. Don't do it.'

Joanna Lumley

———◆◆———

Pentathlete Mary Peters grew up in Northern Ireland and won a gold medal at the Munich Olympics in 1972, at the height of the Troubles. A year later she told Woman's Hour *her intensive training was not enough to take her mind off the situation at home.*

'It's hard to forget because I love Belfast and Ulster. I love the people and I feel so sad that all this is going on, but I think it has helped to inspire me to do what I did in Munich, because I wanted some good news for Northern Ireland.'

Mary Peters

'The problem with female genital mutilation is that it comes in all shapes and sizes. Some of it is simply ceremonial and some of it is devastating. One of the things I have to do as a feminist is take other women's evidence. When Sudanese women tell me they get a great deal out of sex, I cannot tell them they are lying.'

Germaine Greer in a lively discussion with Julie Burchill about her controversial 1999 book, *The Whole Woman*

———◆———

The photograph of a nine-year-old Kim Phuc running naked and terrified from a napalm attack, was the most haunting image of the Vietnam war and won photographer Nick Ut a Pulitzer Prize. Despite suffering horrific burns, Kim survived and in 2000, 28 years after the attack, she spoke to Martha Kearney.

'I still have pain all the time. But in my heart I am free from hatred, from bitterness. I learn that, about the war, it's so wrong and war makes everyone suffer. We need to help each other to move on because we cannot change the past and I think we really need forgiveness and conciliation.'

Kim Phuc

Alison Hargreaves was the first climber to scale the six great north faces of the Alps. In 1993, she talked about the dangers of climbing and whether having two small children – then aged five and two – made her think twice about the risks. Sadly, she was killed two years later while climbing K2.

'If I felt what I was doing was so dangerous and was that risky, then I would actually stop doing it. And obviously, everybody has accidents. But we have accidents doing everything all day. There can be all sorts of things in our daily life that can be fairly risky, and you never know when those risks are going to be. I mean, hopefully, I do tend to minimise the risks involved in climbing, and that's why I carry on.'

Alison Hargreaves

As her father worked for UNESCO, Joan Baez lived in many different countries as a child, including Iraq, where the family lived in Baghdad.

'I was ten and I was very, very ill. I had jaundice and that was the closest I've ever come to dying. The nice thing was that because I was ill, when I started getting better I never had to go back to school and I was able to start my recuperation in the back yard, which meant looking over the mud fence and watching neighbours who lived in mud huts and had nothing. So something in me knew I was getting an education that my friends back in Redlands Junior High School would never get. But part of it was very sad, you know. People were dreadfully poor and we saw all that.'

Joan Baez

Madeleine Albright, the first woman to be appointed Secretary of State in the US, was born in Czechoslovakia but her family were forced to flee after her father found out he was on a Nazi hit list. After returning home they fled again to escape Communism under Soviet rule.

'I truly believe that when the United States is involved it makes a difference and when it isn't, it also makes a difference. So when the US and the Western powers didn't do anything about Hitler, we had to leave Czechoslovakia. And because the United States didn't liberate Czechoslovakia [the USSR did] we had to leave a second time.'

Madeleine Albright, 2001

Angelina Jolie has six children – three adopted and three biological – with ex-husband Brad Pitt. Maddox was adopted from Cambodia, Zahara from Ethiopia and Pax from Vietnam.

'All the kids are learning different languages. I asked them what languages they wanted to learn and Shiloh's learning Kumai, the Cambodian language, Pax is focussing on Vietnamese, Maddox has taken to German and Russian, Zahara is speaking French, Vivienne really wanted to learn Arabic and Knox is learning sign language. I guess you don't know who your children are until they show you who they are and they're just becoming whoever they want to be. It's a bit of my dream, so they are interested in other cultures.'

Angelina Jolie, 2016

Legendary publisher Diana Athill took to writing herself in her latter years and in her book, A Florence Diary, *she detailed a 1947 journey to Italy with a girlfriend which took several days by train.*

'It was much more fun travelling in those days. [After the book was published] I got a letter from a cousin and he said, "It makes me realise what we now miss. We get into an aeroplane and we go 'whoosh' and we arrive whereas your journey was an experience." And it was fun.'

Diana Athill

'We met at drama school and we didn't hit it off immediately. I had spent a year in America, and I'd decided to wear baseball caps and be very loud and say things like, "gross", and "tacky" all the time and "cookie". Jennifer had been in Italy and was being very "refined".

'I came to college later than Jennifer. She'd been there for about a week, and in that week she had managed to get a whole gang together, so by the time I arrived, they just gave me filthy looks from the other side of the canteen, and I knew that I was going to be sent to Coventry for the next three years, which I was.'

Dawn French, in 1986, on meeting her comedy partner Jennifer Saunders

'Two years ago, I did a play, I made two films and three televisions in one year and I thought that was just too much, so we took a six-month trip into the Middle East and learned a little of the situation there in Jordan, Syria. I had been in Egypt and Turkey before, but we went back. We even went into Petra, the Red Rose City, half as old as time. I have only one hobby and that's travelling, but we don't go places unless we can stay long enough to learn something of the people and the country.'

Lillian Gish, 1957

'I was staggered the first time I went to the rugby ... I was very taken aback by the difference in a rugby crowd and a football crowd. And as a woman being at the rugby, it's quite a welcoming place, whereas I can remember going to football matches in London and feeling quite intimidated. So that was obviously a welcome change.

'What's on the pitch is horrible and violent and dreadful, but meanwhile, you're sitting with a lot of people who will happily buy you half a pint and a pie and chat away to you, even if they're supporting the opposition, so I found that rather enjoyable.'

JK Rowling

'We [go back to the Canadian Wilderness] every summer and, in fact, this summer we're doing the first river canoe trip as a family. That means down the river in canoes, through rapids and things.

'We won't do anything really dangerous. Not with children. It involves flying into the location, which is in a wilderness area, therefore no roads, and we'll go with a number of other people, and there will be two people per canoe and we will go for a certain length of time every day and then we will stop and pitch tents and cook around campfires and squash mosquitoes.

'There are still bears, but they usually don't bother you unless they've been around civilisation and are used to people leaving garbage around.'

Margaret Atwood speaking in 1987 about her plans to take her eleven-year-old daughter on a family trip to the Canadian forests where she was raised

'I think Oriental women are much more liberated. They're more independent, they don't have the usual slavery situation as much as in the West. For instance in every town in Japan, they have a dance club where women can go and pick up men. Like Playboy club except the Bunnies are men. And that means there are enough women who are independent enough, financially and morally, that they can go to those places freely.'

Yoko Ono, 1973

————◆◆◆————

'I can't write in English. All the really important things in my life I do in Spanish. Counting, praying, scolding my grandchildren, making love. I would feel ridiculous panting in English.'

Chilean novelist Isabel Allende, 2008

LIFE LESSONS

In seven decades of the show, women of all backgrounds and with wildly different experiences have dispensed nuggets of sage advice for loyal listeners. So here is the Woman's Hour Guide to Life, *as told by our guests.*

'I think knitting is far more useful than a computer. At least you get a sweater out of it.'

Vivienne Westwood, 2014

In 2008, Harry Potter *author JK Rowling gave a speech at Harvard entitled,* The Fringe Benefits of Failure and the Importance of Imagination. *Six years later, during her* Woman's Hour *takeover, she explained the theme.*

'I genuinely sat down and thought, "What do I really wish someone had told me at 21?" and it was that above everything else, that it's impossible to live without failing, unless you live so cautiously that you never do anything, in which case you've failed by default. And I think that would have been a liberating thing to hear from someone who'd had some success, and it would have comforted me when I did hit my own quite substantial failures, which I did in my twenties.'

JK Rowling

'The daughter of a woman who's been sexually abused tends to inherit the guilt. The child who has been abused feels that it must have been her fault, even though it never is, of course. It's always, "Well, I must have said no the wrong way or not strongly enough, or I must have been asking for it," because developmentally that's what children do. And you feel guilt for it and it usually turns into body hatred, hatred of your body, self-mutilation. I have lived with body issues and body self-hatred all my life and that's one of the reasons why, I think.'

Actress Jane Fonda, who revealed in 2014 that her mother, Frances Ford Seymour, had been sexually abused from the age of eight. Frances took her own life when Jane was eight

---

'The more famous one becomes the harder one has to work. I've found that to maintain or surpass a standard is much harder than to arrive at it.'

Opera superstar Dame Joan Sutherland, 1959

'You have a choice. You can leave this world, which is the awful way to go. You leave your children, you leave all that you love. Or you can stay and fight for everything. I think women do that anyway, don't we? I mean, to be pregnant and to give birth is a fight and it's very painful, and when you do have your children you adore them and you worship them. Certainly you're not going to leave just because life is difficult and tragic.

'I believe in fighting and I don't admire people that are weak. So I have survived those reverses in my life. I have paid off all my debts, and my children are well today, I'm happily married today, so life is good and I think, to all women, we just have to have the strength God gives to us and to stay in there and fight all the way.'

Screen legend Debbie Reynolds on how she kept going after ex-husband Harry Karl saddled her with $2 million of debts

———◆◆◆———

'I was trained from kindergarten not to be a team player.'

Journalist and TV presenter Anne Robinson

'I find it quite easy to shut [the fame] out. I'm an ordinary person, you know. I wasn't a showbiz person, I was a photographer and just a person, I haven't been brought up in the showbiz world, I didn't start young in the public eye. So I like truth, you know, I like just being ordinary.

'I grew up with good values. I think that's a lot to do with it. I'm not necessarily a materialistic person. My values are more earthy things, so I don't find it too hard. Hopefully I won't find it hard. It's easy to say that now, but you don't know what the future will bring.'

Linda McCartney on living with superstar Paul

'Being old and wise and being a grandmother now, I know that some things attract exact results and if you are out very late at night, if you are very drunk, if you are unsure of how to get home and you are unsuitably dressed for staggering about, you are very vulnerable. I hate to say it because I'd love to say that everyone can wear exactly what they want but that isn't life. I'm trying to say as an old hand, who has been a girl who wore miniskirts in the sixties, that I've been there but I'm trying to say to people, be careful because that way all kinds of horrors lie.'

Actress Joanna Lumley gives advice to young women on drinking, in 2013

———◆·◆·◆———

'I was always brought up to believe that whatever you are doing you should do the best you can, in whatever that activity is. So I think it was that belief that you can do, and whatever you're doing make sure you're aiming to do your best.'

Prime Minister Theresa May

'The sixties was about love and peace and a lot of us of the Baby Boomers generation did care about our children and what we did is show the next generation how to express love. Also, for women particularly, you could have a future, you could have a profession, you were sexually liberated. It was a huge liberating time.'

Actress Julie Walters, 2012

'All I know is I am terribly brutalised inside. I know my soul is scarred. I know I am bleeding inside all the time. I know the pain of my people's suffering, the pain of having a husband behind bars for twenty-five years, the pain of bringing up children under the atmosphere I brought them up, is so great inside. But what has happened is that it hasn't brutalised me to an extent of being consumed in hate.'

Activist Winnie Mandela, former wife of Nelson Mandela, reflects on raising her children while dealing with constant scrutiny and abuse from the South African government during her husband's internment

'The thing that I pass on to her the most is "Don't rush at everything." There's that thing in your late teens and early twenties when you think "I must have a mortgage". I think I did a bit, I don't know why because I came from a very liberal household. So that would be my thing to her. Don't rush.'

Kate Beckinsale on advice to her seventeen-year-old daughter Lily, 2016

———————

'Underneath my sophisticated exterior there is a moron.'

Comedian and writer Ruby Wax, 2016

———————

'[I had] the father who always made me feel fat, and who I never felt could love me unless I was perfect. So I spent most of my adult life trying to be perfect so men would love me but, of course, we're not meant to be perfect. We're meant to be complete.'

Actress Jane Fonda, on father Henry Fonda, talking in 2005

*At the age of 18, with little movie experience, ingénue Debbie
Reynolds was chosen to star in* Singin' in the Rain *opposite
Gene Kelly. After three months of intensive training on a studio
sound stage, the pressure was getting to her.*

'I was crying under the piano and everyone had gone to
lunch, and some legs appeared in front of my face, and
I'm sobbing away, and a voice said, "What is it, little girl?
What's the matter?" And I said, "Well, I can't learn all this.
This is impossible," and tears were streaming down my
face. And it was Fred Astaire and when he saw it was me
he pulled me out and he said I could watch him rehearse,
and I did, and I saw how tough it was for him and how
frustrated he got. He threw his cane, he broke his cane,
he cursed at the drummer, he had a terrible time of it.
He looked at me with madness in his eyes and I crept out
the door because it was equally as hard for Mr Astaire
who was a great, brilliant dancer as it was for this little
frustrated creature underneath the piano.'

Debbie Reynolds

'I can't be bothered with people who have no sense of humour in life. Life is too short for those people, those flat-footed, boring, dreary, ancient, dry as dust people who think that men are allowed to write about sex but women aren't. That men are allowed to have sex but women aren't. I'm bored with them.'

Erica Jong, 2014

———————◆◆◆———————

'I've never liked my acting very much. I never liked myself very much. When I see it many, many years later I am able to separate myself from it but I've never been terribly enamoured with myself. I've never been totally satisfied with anything I did which is good and you'd better stay that way. The day you are totally satisfied with yourself, you stop trying.'

Hollywood star Bette Davis

'I've already been a has-been. By fourteen, which isn't easy to accomplish. But I managed to do it. So that was fun. But actually, in all seriousness, it was kind of a relief because it made me so grateful for what life has brought me since then. And very humbled. And very aware of every fortunate thing that happens to me since. I think every person in their profession has that fear that one day it's all going to go away. But when it actually does, you're left to realise you will survive.'

Former child star Drew Barrymore speaking in 2007 about her fall from grace as a teenager, before reviving her Hollywood career in her twenties

———◆———

In 1986, after eight years in exile, Benazir Bhutto was preparing to return to Pakistan when she spoke to Woman's Hour *about fears for her safety.*

'Let's say that there are always apprehensions in life, and certainly there are apprehensions even now in my mind. But I don't think one should ever be scared of life, and I've always believed in meeting challenges head-on.'

After two terms as Prime Minister, Benazir Bhutto was assassinated in Pakistan in 2007

Rabbi Julia Neuberger is the daughter of a German-Jewish mother who was forced to flee Nazi persecution in 1937. Forty years later, she recalled her own visit to post-war Germany.

'The first time I went, I had considerable difficulty going. I was tremendously conscious of persecution of Jews in Germany and tremendously conscious of my own background which I suppose most of the time I'm not. I speak German relatively fluently and it made it very difficult because in some sense I felt quite German while I was there. But after a bit, one tends to ignore that situation. One starts off being prejudiced against anyone over the age of 55 thinking, "I wonder what you were doing in the War" and then one ends up saying, "No, that's not a fair thing to wonder, not a fair thing to ask." In fact one should just try to get to know the people as individuals.'

Rabbi Julia Neuberger

'[*The Good Ship Lollipop*] had a beginning, a middle and an end and it had a happy ending. In life you make your own way and you try to do better for other people but there is no script. I don't know what the ending's going to be but I've certainly been a fortunate woman in my life.'

**Former actress and US ambassador
Shirley Temple Black**

'I still have to work so hard to extract that [confident] persona. I have been so fortunate in my life and I've had so many good experiences but I never feel that far away from the eleven-year-old girl who always stepped right out of her shoes.'

Actress Sigourney Weaver

'They say that we all would like to commit a crime, we all have a crime in us and thus it's done for us vicariously or it's a catharsis. It gets rid of these feelings of violence and anger. And also there is the theory that we all feel a sort of pleasure at other people's misfortunes, a sort of schadenfreude. It's a very unpleasant thing but I think nevertheless it's true so this way you can be sitting very warm and comfortable and safe and read about pretty horrific unsafe things happening to other people with absolute impunity.'

Novelist Ruth Rendell, in 1979, on what draws readers to crime fiction

'Both my parents always said that everyone is the artifice of their own good fortune, and they made it absolutely clear that every single one of us has been given a gift and it's our job, basically, to take that gift, hone it, and then use it for the benefit of other people. That was drummed into you that that's what you had to do. And there was no point saying that you didn't have a talent because that was denying what God had given you.'

QC and Labour peer, Baroness Scotland

———◆◆◆———

'I count to ten before I say things sometimes ... I've seen people on television get cross and angry. Then they say things that they wish they hadn't said and certainly they are then at a disadvantage. If you're really to assess the problems in front of you, you ought to keep calm. You don't make the best decisions if you get agitated about something.'

Margaret Thatcher, 1976

'I used to cry. And then there came a point when, just to get rid of [ex-partner Malcom McLaren], I just turned the tap on. And after that, I have found that I've been almost unable to cry for anybody because I think when you stop crying for yourself then you stop crying for the most terrible thing that could happen [even though] you can put yourself in their shoes.

'So I stopped crying, but I do care very much about people's suffering. It touches me more than anything. That's why I fight.'

Dame Vivienne Westwood, 2014

———◆———

'That movie [*Fatal Attraction*] and that character have had a very, very positive effect because it got people talking about things they hadn't been talking about. It uncovered this strange anger and insecurity that I think has been kind of latent in our society, probably brought on by the '60s and never resolved.'

Glenn Close on playing 'bunny boiler'
Alex Forrest in the 1988 movie

'My grandmother used to say, "Gertie, you must grow up able to turn your hand to anything. Remember there's no such word as 'can't'." I was brought up on a whole lot of those old adages – "Where there's a will there's a way," "Never say die" and "If at first you don't succeed … " I kicked against them as a child but many's the time they have become very handy since I've grown up.'

Actress Gertrude Lawrence, 1949

'I went to school just before the First World War and, one evening, when I was spending the holidays at our home in the Midlands, a business friend of my father's came to tea. He asked me how I was getting on at school, and I was too young to realise he was just being patronising and polite. So I plunged into an exciting description of my ambition to be a writer and my longing to be given some really responsible work.

'He soon interrupted my prattle with a devastating remark. "My dear child," he said. "Surely you don't imagine that anyone would put real confidence in one of you sex."'

***Testament of Youth* author Vera Brittain, 1953**

'Sometimes I paid a pretty high price for it but on the whole I did it my way and I have very few regrets. I did pay a price because I didn't get all the jobs I thought I should have got, but what did come true for me was spectacular so I really have nothing to quibble about.'

Bette Midler, 2014

'Let's face it, the pattern of English life, whether it be in school or out of it, can be something rather dull. Something that makes little appeal to the imagination. Whether it's the climate or the price we pay for having such good character in other ways, I don't know.'

Author Iris Murdoch, 1957

'I wanted to go on the stage. I loved cooking but I was mad on Shakespeare and I did get a chance to go into Oldham Repertory, I was going to be Lady Macbeth. So when I had a chance to give up a good job as a home economist to go on this risky stage thing, everybody said, "Oh your poor widowed mother! Oh you couldn't do that." And it was my poor widowed mother who said, "Take it! If you don't do it you will spend your life regretting it."

Marguerite Patten, 2009

'It was part of our upbringing that you just had to do your best. It was also very much a part of one's upbringing that what mattered was what a person was. It wasn't the background that you came from at all but your character that mattered. And you had to develop that and you had to do unto others as you'd expect them to do to you. You were expected to make your own way. You were expected to do the best with whatever talents and abilities you had and in a way it was rather a sin not to. There was a strong streak of duty.'

Margaret Thatcher, then leader of the Conservative Party, in 1976

'There's no recipe for resilience. Life is a place where terrible things can happen to people that can destroy them.'

Poet Liz Lochhead, 2016

———◦•◦•◦———

'A Superwoman is not in my opinion a woman who can do everything or who tries to do everything. I think these sorts of people are a pain in the neck. A Superwoman is somebody who specifically doesn't try too much, who knows her own limitations and sticks within them.'

Shirley Conran, author of the bestselling *Superwoman*

———◦•◦•◦———

In 1980, Joan Collins' nine-year-old daughter Katyana Kass was hit by a car and spent months in a coma. The public responded with thousands of letters of support as Joan kept a hopeful vigil by her daughter's side.

'What was repeated constantly throughout the letters I received was, "Never give up." That has been my credo since then and it was a bit before. I do believe you should never give up on something that you believe in. It's a very good piece of advice.'

Joan Collins

In 1999, a year after her infamous affair with President Clinton, Monica Lewinsky talked to Jenni Murray about the effect of the fallout on her family.

'My father is a radiation oncologist and we've all, in my family, reminded ourselves almost every day in this past year that what we're going through is not more difficult than someone who's facing a terminal illness.'

Monica Lewinsky

———◆◆◆———

'Philosophy is like plumbing. There is a system of ideas running under the world that we live in and we don't notice it a great deal of the time, any more than we notice the water. Then sometimes awful smells start coming up from below or the taps don't run. You've got to take up the floorboards and see what's wrong.'

Philosopher Professor Mary Midgley, 2003

'My situation typifies the women of this age, in that we have to be very many things and we have very many labels. I am a housewife and I am married to John and at the same time I am an artist and a mother too.'

Yoko Ono, artist and wife of John Lennon, 1973

'While I'm a great admirer of the strong, silent male type, I find women who are overly stoical a little unsettling. Other groups of oppressed people can list the wrongs that have been done to them but if a woman tries this she will probably go insane as A) it's been happening forever and B) it never ends. Faced with such a history of non-stop atrocities how can any broad never get a tiny bit cross? To me a woman who looks at the world with calm eyes and an equitable temper has something of the Stepford Wife about her.'

Julie Burchill, 2016

'My parents dragged us kicking and screaming to Hebrew school and I must say we didn't take to it very well. We didn't get much out of it. We got "do unto others". That was really important. That's all we got but I do believe that's all you need. That's what they're all peddling and it's a good thing so I took it to heart.'

Bette Midler, 2014

WOMEN OF THE HOUR: LIST OF CONTRIBUTORS

Rogers, Ginger 79, 176
Rook, Jean 17, 113
Roosevelt, Eleanor 168
Rowling, JK 3, 11, 90, 100, 218, 222
Rubinstein, Helge 109

Sanders, Deidre 110, 116
Scotland, Baroness 15, 51, 146, 166, 169, 234
Shapiro, Helen 9, 128
Shriver, Lionel 200
Shulman, Alexandra 138, 177
Simon, Carly 80, 81
Simone, Nina 28
Stark, Freya 16, 209
Streep, Meryl 141
Summerskill, Edith 52, 138
Sutherland, Dame Joan 223

Temple Black, Shirley 50, 70, 82, 143, 232

Thatcher, Margaret 18, 20, 37, 95, 135, 154, 164, 234, 238
Twiggy 12, 94, 99

Walters, Barbara 47, 144
Walters, Julie 227
Warner, Marina 84, 184
Warnock, Dame Mary 55
Wax, Ruby 50, 88
Weaver, Sigourney 11, 146, 190, 233
Weldon, Fay 48, 139
Westwood, Dame Vivienne 15, 70, 93, 96, 162, 222, 235
Williams, Baroness Shirley 27, 39, 41, 64, 109, 114, 115, 124, 130
Winfrey, Oprah 25, 38, 89, 143, 181
Winslet, Kate 10, 92
Wood, Victoria 209